The Will to Consciousness

The Will to Consciousness

NICOLAS LEHOUX

© 2019 Nicolas Lehoux
Montréal (Québec, Canada)

Lehoux, Nicolas

The Will to Consciousness

ISBN : 9781082204609

nicolaslehoux.com

1

I will myself to consciousness. It is a decision that concerns me and me alone. I believe this is the only way I can remain in an awakened state; so I journey into the infinite without looking back, without compromise and without ulterior motive.

2

The only way to be truly alive is to be willfully conscious. It has to become a fixation. Everything brings me back to this desire. Living in a willfully conscious way allows me to see the world through the eyes of the Living God. This perspective, rich and glorious as it is, gives me the strength to face the truth, as painful as it may be.

3

To be willfully conscious is to surrender to what I Truly Am, to fully manifest my consciousness. This may seem simple at first glance, but once you dedicate yourself to it, you quickly run up against the general law that today's moral majority considers the norm. To live like this, at crosscurrent, you can't be afraid of being mocked. In fact, you can't be afraid of anything, which is an indication that you have nothing left to lose.

4

Consciousness, as a realm of manifestation, creates a limited context like that of the visible world so that it may become conscious of itself. Limits allow it to better experience its infinite nature, like a reflection in a mirror. The individual who is willfully conscious experiences his own consciousness; he feels it vibrate, then, through an unnatural act, fixes it in the relative by all means possible. But the general law is there to keep him from it by making sure he remains asleep. It takes a strong will to defy the general law. For those with nothing left to lose, only consciousness matters.

5

The one who is willfully conscious is no longer just a pawn in a chess game; he has, through an unnatural act, freed himself from it and observes the game from the perspective of the Observer. He plays the game in his own way, neither pawn, nor player. He is content to be. The world whirls around him but doesn't disturb him.

6

He who is willfully conscious toils to stay vigilant even during the interminable plateaus that may characterize his human life. These plateaus are major obstacles because they are, indeed, a component to the general law. Their monotony may cause him to lose his vigilance. At these times it behooves him to create ways to make his life more dynamic—to incite change when necessary. He is aware that routine kills genius, so he must know how to move on wisely without being attached to the past. Though concerned about the future he lives centered in the here and now.

7

The eventful and busy times are not the most dangerous for the one who is willfully conscious, but rather those periods when routine lulls him into relaxing his vigilance. If you drop a frog into a pot of water and slowly bring it to a boil, it won't feel the difference in temperature, and, little by little, it will surrender instead of leaping from its casket to safety. Such is the life of those who prefer comfort and stability. They slowly fall asleep, forgetting they are prisoners, until they completely abdicate. They are dead before even having begun to live.

8

A warrior and a soldier are not the same. The latter is asleep and follows orders without thought. The warrior, on the other hand, is his own master. He rarely fights. Because he is willfully conscious, he is elsewhere when the tiger passes.

9

The warrior lives in the here and now. He is free from his own past; he has burned all those bridges. His gaze is turned inward, from which he sees all, effortlessly, through the panoptic of his thoughts. If he is concerned about his future, it is only to give himself direction, like the backbone does in the human body. He doesn't live in this future, but rather in the infinity of possibilities that present themselves to his free consciousness. The warrior lives in a willfully conscious manner; it's the only way he can be attentive to all the signs that allow him to stay centered on the essential.

10

To live in a willfully conscious way calls for a healthy dose of audacity. It is imperative to push back limits unrelentingly so as not to fall into routine and lose vigilance.

11

To be face-to-face with myself is where I want to be so that a perfect connection can exist between my self and my Being. To live consciously is to juxtapose my Being with my self in an infinite dance where I turn continually inward, while renewing myself each second.

12

Even if he stares at a blank wall for hours, the one who lives in a willfully conscious way is never bored because he is in touch with the invisible. He knows when and what someone thinks of him. He perceives subtle details that are invisible to the common man. While the one who is asleep may feel like he will go insane by doing nothing, the man who is willfully conscious jumps for joy at the occasion. He takes advantage of the moment to be attentive to his feelings and impressions. He emerges from this period of silence expanded and inspired, while the one who is asleep feels like he wasted his time.

13

The sleeping are barriers to those who wish to shed limits and live consciously. They irritate me at times, but in the end, I know that in spite of their best efforts they facilitate things for me on the subtle levels of consciousness. By challenging me incessantly, they force me to stay vigilant and attentive. I could, of course, leave society and lock myself away in a monastery, but if I did, I would feel only half alive. I would be concentrating on a primordial aspect of my consciousness, but I would miss its essence.

14

You have to be able to handle anything the cyclone of life hurls at you if you want to stay awake in the city. The chaos of the modern world does not perturb the one who lives in a willfully conscious way because he is anchored in the abundance of the infinite. Is there anything more difficult than staying centered on the essential while sitting at the core of a maelstrom that incessantly threatens to engulf you?

15

To take everything means to pursue all my desires and satisfy them. For this I must forgo morality and trust in my own ethics.

16

Thanks to his personal ethics, the one who lives in a willfully conscious way follows his Being, like a plumb line that points invariably toward the center of the Earth. If he rejects morality, it's because it herds the masses toward conformity, toward the basest common denominator. Morality is a general law that opposes all forms of individuation. Like the universe, whose physical laws don't apply in a black hole, enlightenment is nowhere and everywhere at the same time, and doesn't follow the general law. A black hole, like the enlightened one, has its own laws that are based neither on the opinions of others, nor on what is considered normal.

17

Awakening is an unnatural act. I felt most strongly I was defying the general law after I had a vasectomy. I thumbed my nose at my evolutionary warm-blooded mammal nature, that which has as its be-all and end-all to reproduce and never lift its head to ask the real question: "Am I here as a cog in the evolutionary machine, or to realize my true nature, which is something else entirely?" By getting a vasectomy, I answered the question once and for all. I lifted my head and embraced the higher path. I chose myself instead of investing time and energy in others who were starting at zero. Some find me egotistical: I call it being centered. I have understood that at the subtlest levels of reality, we don't beget children in this primitive way. There are, in fact, other ways to create life.

18

For me, the vasectomy was a willfully conscious act of liberation. I knew that nothing would be the same afterward. No longer having to worry about involuntarily inseminating a woman helps me see them as individuals rather than breeders. Now I can participate in enlightening sex, which has nothing to do with the procreative act that brutish man shares with animals. The vasectomy—unnatural act that it is—liberated me from my animal nature.

19

All unnatural acts lead toward a willfully conscious life. It is by sprinkling my life with acts that fly in the face of the general law that I have the best chance of crystalizing in me a permanent center of gravity. Why? Because nature is stupid and doomed. It is the symbol for all that is ephemeral and impermanent, while enlightenment is a permanent state that has no use for time and space.

20

To constantly ask myself what the majority thinks—and do the opposite—is the only way I can remain in the truth. When a mass of people move in a direction, it creates a slipstream. I could fall in behind and let myself be dragged along, but I've realized that this mass of sleepers is controlled by greater powers that do everything possible to have them conform and forget what is essential. It's therefore in paddling against the flow like a man possessed that I can stay awake, because there are no wayposts or user manuals. I create myself each second. I am ready to break the mold and start afresh—such is the confidence I have in my own creativity.

21

It is by creating myself without compromise that I Am. I don't let others define who I am because resisting the general law as much as possible is conducive to staying willfully conscious.

22

My creative work allows me to live consciously because it ensures that I do not forget myself. It is the mirror that allows me to realize my true nature and embody it in the world. By following my predisposition, which is that of an artist, I encourage in me the feeling of being at the right place at the right time, of being in harmony with that which I have resolved to be. And that is why, when I chose to get a vasectomy, I made a pact with myself to devote myself unconditionally to that which is permanent.

23

To live in a willfully conscious way implies knowing what is essential for you. If having children is a must, then you should do it freely and with joy. By raising them consciously you will be able to live consciously in turn. If, however, it is essential for you to dedicate yourself to individuation, then pursue that without hesitation or compromise. Some will say that if everybody was to follow the latter path, the life cycle on Earth would be disrupted. This is obvious to me, but life on Earth does not necessarily represent the apogee of development. I remain convinced that in worlds where peace and immortality reign, there is no longer the need to reproduce in such a crude manner.

24

I feel a light growing inside me. My conscious life began the day I touched my center and reached the source I had always sensed was there. I had to dig deep but I invested all of my intelligence and passion in it. When I touched this source, the light rose and slaked my thirst for the absolute. Ever since, this source continues to surprise me with its purity and beauty. I became a thinking light and this light began emanating from me.

25

I am this light that emanates from the depths of my Being. I am unflinchingly convinced of it. From the day I synthesized the knowledge that led me toward enlightenment I ceased doing and began Being. This is very subtle, and for the majority there is no difference between the two. But for the one who lives in a willfully conscious way, everything resides in perceptible subtlety. My psyche awoke to reveal a new world to me, a world that had been there all along: the invisible.

26

There is in each of us an inexhaustible source of light. Very few have the determination to awaken it and honor it. One must be, in fact, ready to lose everything to enter eternal life.

27

The awakened source of light bestows upon me a surprising clarity that allows me to live in a willfully conscious way. I will never forget the experience when I finally pierced the fine veil that separated me from the absolute. It was my last day as a human being. I made of myself a living suicide and took charge of my destiny. Since that day, I have looked at the world through the eyes of the Living God. I realized that the only viable option for me was to live in a willfully conscious way. I entered the truth to never emerge.

28

The one who awakens on the Earthly plane should not expect to be understood—rather the opposite. Enlightenment is always the exception and the general law does not appreciate its presence. So be it! It's too late, and the radical shift that takes place at the center of his Being is irreversible. So the general law has no choice but to turn against those who want to connect with him.

29

Awakening is painful, and yet I am so vast that the pain does not reach the depths of my Being. I may be nervous and worry, but at my core lies a profound calm that nobody and nothing has troubled until now.

30

It's painful to go unnoticed even in the eyes of those who claim to be devoted to enlightenment. They have a preconceived notion of what an enlightened master should look like: asexual, clad in robes and sickeningly humble. And because I am still young, have not renounced the world and don't sport a long white beard, I lack credibility. In truth, it matters little. I don't need others' approbation to validate what I Am. You won't see me renounce the world because others have a preconceived idea that an enlightened master should do so. Personally, I intend having relations with as many women as I can, go to the gym, make money and enjoy myself as much as possible. In fact, I am determined to continue living like all Westerners around me. The only difference is that I will do it in a willfully conscious way.

31

In the Western world of this early twenty-first century, it is impossible to live in a willfully conscious way. The one who does so lives under the law of exception. The general law ensures that nobody can awaken, but a few individuals do manage to slip through the cracks. It can be a living hell for them when they realize they are alone in this world and that nobody really has the will to change radically. Living in a willfully conscious manner is inaccessible to humans—very few can claim to have established this state in themselves. A human is a soulless machine. There is nothing inside—neither God, nor soul—and when he dies he has no chance of attaining immortality. To do so, he would have to crystalize the awakened state in himself while alive so that by the time of death he has made a habit of living in eternity.

32

Only he who allows himself to Be can pursue the willfully conscious life. The Living God recognizes that consciousness is his most permanent quality. To latch on to it becomes his only viable option.

33

I applied myself to the study of what others before me said about this state we call "enlightenment." I pored over all traditions and found that, beneath the surface, they had a common core. It was while reading Aldous Huxley's The

Perennial Philosophy that I understood there had to be a common thread running through the various definitions and techniques leading to enlightenment. I reached an all-encompassing perspective of the traditions, which I then synthesized to be able to integrate my knowledge into a concrete way of life. I unraveled religious symbolism to get to this common core that led me to my center. In that moment, I awoke something powerful. I felt like I had done the impossible, that I had arrived. I stopped searching because I had found the absolute. All I had to do was integrate the experience in the world without losing myself in the immensity of what I Am. From that point on, to live in a willfully conscious manner was no longer an option, but an obligation.

34

The one who knows to look inside himself for answers understands that knowledge is not something that is learned. He may learn things through study, but the essential need not be studied. An individual can awaken without having gone to school.

35

What I do best, nobody taught me. I learned, like a primate would, to mimic my fellow creatures to be able to live in the world, but for me happiness is innate. I am joy. In other words, I did not learn to live in a willfully conscious manner, I gave myself permission to do so. I surrender myself to be what I Am by forgetting society's programs and concentrating on the essential.

36

It is through writing that I obtain the best vantage points on the world and on myself. They are there in me, ready to manifest. I know things I did not even imagine I knew. Is this learned ignorance? No matter how we define this source of inexhaustible knowledge, my only desire is to cultivate it.

37

Being willfully conscious, I have access to knowledge. I know what I have to do every second. I don't think we can reduce this to simple intuition. It's much more than that. It's direct access to a universal data base which is available to me as long as I remain in harmony and centered. Only then, perched high on the summit of my Being, can I spy the entire world. I found the panoptic that gives me access to everything I want to know. Nothing is out of my grasp. A question contains its own answer, otherwise it is not a real question.

38

To be willfully conscious is to be in harmony with what I have set out to be. It is to be attentive to all details in order to appreciate them for their true value. When you have access to the Great All you need profound discrimination.

39

I do not pretend to know everything. Of what benefit is that, anyway? I know what I need to know to remain harmonious. If I lack some knowledge, I meet a teacher or I have the intuition to teach myself. I do not encumber my mind with the superfluous. I have a lot of respect for myself. If I learn, it is for the pleasure of it and I never forget that I already have a grasp of the essential, that happiness is the most permanent state and if I live it in full consciousness, chances are this state will outlive me. This state is more my self than myself.

40

In life, the plateaus are the most difficult to bear. Monotony sets in, automatisms develop and this false security incites us to be less attentive because we think we already know what will happen. Plateaus are a daunting challenge to the willfully conscious life because they provide multitude opportunities to retreat to the commonplace. When everything moves at speed—when life is full to the brim—our focus is essential and all our senses are on alert. Plateaus, on the other hand, make us negligent and torpid. It therefore behooves us to constantly develop effective strategies to stimulate our attention because the conscious life is the only one that really matters.

41

There is nothing to be done when I plateau. It seems everything conspires to prevent me from getting out of it. I may take action, take steps, try to renew myself, but it is in vain, because the plateau is a normal phase of all development. I learned to appreciate it while still giving myself the means to not fall asleep under the weight of monotony.

42

The plateau is the challenge of the enlightened one. At any moment he can be overwhelmed by ecstasy and lose touch with the material world. This is not dramatic in itself because the planetary context is rudimentary and coarse, but nevertheless, my conception of the willfully conscious life implies being wholly present at all levels of reality. I felt at one point in my life that the absolute had become so important to me that I was slowly losing my connection with the Earthly plane. So I made the decision to return to the world and took the appropriate measures to get there. It is possible to plateau even in the absolute because it is so vast and I end up surrendering myself to it.

43

To live in a willfully conscious manner, you cannot rely on others to help you. It must be an individual, uncompromising aspiration because on this planet hardly anyone has that true desire. I meet many people who seem to be on the path, but in reality none of them are willing to lose everything in order to attain a conscious life. The attraction of the outside world is stronger than the ideal of awakening. I am not afraid to lose everything because I have found in me a source of light independent of the outside world. Even if I lost all my possessions, I could continue to create. You cannot take away my inner world and my creativity. That's why I am happy. My happiness does not depend on the goodwill of others.

44

I am presently crossing a plateau. I currently live in a Montreal neighborhood called Le Plateau, which is rather symbolic. All my efforts to make my creative work known are weakened by the general law. At times, I have the impression that my attempts to attain public notoriety are being slowed down deliberately. And since my life is so calm, it is more difficult for me to remain willfully conscious. I understand, however, that it is a good idea to surround myself with people who also desperately want to live in a willfully conscious way. It is thanks to Ouspensky's book, In Search of the Miraculous: Fragments of an Unknown Teaching, that I realized how important this is. For several years now, I have been working to create an enlightenment community. So, in spite of this appalling plateau which never ceases, I manage to maintain my willfully conscious state for I surround myself with other bedlamites of the conscious life.

45

To live in a willfully conscious way in a context where the dominant majority live unconsciously is an insurmountable, or better yet, impossible challenge, and yet I succeed with flying colors. I have met very few people who are as thirsty for the absolute as I am. Most desire it as an afterthought without ever really doing what is necessary to quench this most normal of thirsts once and for all.

46

I endeavor through my projects and actions to attract the attention of those few who, like me, desire to live in a willfully conscious way. I have already done the impossible by finding enough of them to create an organization that, in a concrete way, aims to teach a way of life that encourages conscious living. To live in this way, a context is required that is not only conducive to the emergence of the feeling of enlightenment, but also to its practical support over time. It is precisely during more monotonous periods that this type of community is essential. There is always someone in the group to remind me that I am sinking into routine. I long sought the means of founding such a community. Of course, the one I founded will not suit everyone, but that's not what matters. What is important is that I am able to clearly identify those with whom I share a core essence, and that together we provide a concrete context that allows us to live in a willfully conscious manner.

47

Being willfully conscious in a world that is asleep is sometimes tedious and painful. Although I may have a profound view of the world, opportunities to share my point of view are rare. There seems to be a conspiracy to collectively undershoot the essential. For example, a super hurricane destroyed part of New York last month—three days before the presidential elections. The media went on and on about the "hurricane of the century" and the president's effort to help the victims, but nowhere was it mentioned that this hurricane had been created from scratch using technology still unknown to the public. I was in a rage, but found no outlet except through a violent flu. I was helpless to do anything else, defenseless in the face of the sordid machinations of the manipulative plutocratic system. It is an all-too-familiar feeling to have these clear perceptions and nobody with whom to share them.

48

The feeling of helplessness that sometimes grips me is fortunately counterbalanced by the knowledge that there is nothing to do, that the world is a representation within my consciousness. The world is a realm of manifestation that allows me to be willfully conscious. The impact of these contradictory feelings weighs on me heavily at times. Though I may be the Living God, some days I think more than I Am.

49

The feeling of helplessness in the face of the world's immensity is what ultimately makes me capitulate. I am not a savior, nor a messiah, that is not my function in this world. By saving myself, by freeing myself, I set an example and that is enough. Why should I make myself sick because the majority of humans are sheep and the few shepherds who lead them to the slaughterhouse have no qualms about mistreating them and stealing from them before they die? I do sometimes become all too human and forget that all this is but a film, but it doesn't last long because living in a willfully conscious way has become a habit. I can, in fact, relax my attention for a while because the systems I deftly put in place in my life, like art, inevitably bring me back to the conscious life.

50

I am resigned to no longer doing anything. I let everything happen in me. It's subtle, but it works. It makes things easier for me. If I look at my life as a whole, I realize that I have always favored ease. Even when I was receiving social assistance and had almost no money, I never felt that life was hard. Everything works out because I am in the right place at the right time. I have often run headlong into prejudices and lack of understanding, and though this still happens, it disturbs me less and less. I do not seek others' approval because it's usually impossible to obtain, anyway. It's easy to be a revolutionary when you're in school and have no responsibilities. You see a person for who they truly are only once they've become an adult. The most original ones quickly become average and insipid. In my case, however, I really tried to apply the first sentence of this paragraph, to firmly grasp its essence. I applied myself to doing nothing... unless I felt inspired. The nearly ten years I spent on social assistance provided me with all the time I needed. And if I was so prolific in my creative work, it is not because I felt obliged to do it, but because I let it happen in me effortlessly.

51

I have experienced times when my mind was completely silent. Even during those moments, I was able to perceive this irreducible factor, which is consciousness. It was then that I realized that my consciousness did not need my self to Be. It needs it to perceive itself, like a mirror, but it can do without it. Willful consciousness is a state that surpasses my self immeasurably. It demands absolute trust in my Being. My self is so limited that I would be lost were I not able to perceive that I am much more than Nicolas Lehoux. I have innumerable parallel lives that I can tap into at my leisure to learn more easily. For example, by realizing that I am a gypsy in a parallel life, it is easier for me to learn Spanish and salsa. I realize that instead of learning something external to me, I can know it internally. In this way feelings come to me that recall life experiences. I do this in my art. I enter myself and come out with infinite knowledge that often surprises me. Unlike those who are channels, I appropriate this knowledge. I don't consider that it originates from an entity other than me that uses me as a channel, but rather from my Being, which is more my self than myself.

52

The conscious life cannot be integrated without first being experienced. The first time I experienced it, I felt the existence of something even though my mind had stopped. It didn't scare me; I was not afraid of dying. Such an experience makes it possible to relativize the world. There are many atheists today. For them, there is nothing beyond this world. This is absurd to me, given the repeated experiences I have had that have shown me that beyond Nicolas Lehoux exists consciousness. The latter is infinite, while my self is finite. It is a given that my self is doomed, like everything else in nature. Life itself presupposes death. But consciousness has nothing to do with life. Living in a willfully conscious way is an unnatural act.

53

Consciousness is misunderstood today. Materialists believe that it is only a secretion of the brain. My immaterialist experiences make this hypothesis unlikely. I bathed in the absolute; I surrendered myself to be one with the Great All. These are experiences of a rare depth. I might not have come back had my creative work not been of such vital importance to me. I have deactivated my person (from the Latin persona, meaning "mask") but my work allows me to be fully conscious while still remembering what my self is. By eclipsing my self, I realized that, despite everything, something vast remained. I knew intuitively that this is what the Great Initiates call consciousness.

54

Every day I look at the world through the eyes of the Living God. It's become a habit. My physical eyes are not the only ones at work. I activated my third eye and it works in symbiosis with the other two. Even before I started living consciously, my vocation as artist helped me develop an exceptional way of seeing. I remember when I first arrived in Montreal, I wrote a short poem in which I pointed out that I no longer wanted to listen (to others) but to See (by myself)—see the world as it is without filters imposed by others, without listening to what others think. I wanted to make up my own mind. So I rearranged my world. I refused to enter the labor market and simply observed the world. I drew every day. I always carried my notebook and pencils. I sketched people in parks, in cafes, in the streets. I was teaching my eyes to See. I stopped using words in my comic strips and began to perceive the world more simply without the filter of words that made me so rational. I understand better now—I was intuitively training myself to live in a willfully conscious way.

55

Drawing as much as I did during my adolescence and early adult life taught me to integrate the creative aspect of my personality. Because I create something beautiful every day, I have come to understand that since this beauty emanates from me, I am beautiful.

56

When you do observational drawing, you must forget your own interpretation of the subject in order to really focus on the object you want to draw. In this way it is good training for living consciously because you must put your mind aside to reproduce the model as accurately as possible. This demands your entire attention; you have to be fully absorbed by the task. This strikes me as strangely similar to the willfully conscious mindset that I deal with in this book. And I can see how the thousands of hours spent sketching helped me attain one-pointed focus and not be distracted by anything.

57

Observational drawing helps you see reality as it is, without embellishing it, without bypassing it, without interpreting it. To succeed in reproducing it as it is you must put yourself in a state of extreme receptivity. You have to really see what you are drawing instead of taking only a part of it and filling in the rest with your imagination. To live in a willfully conscious way also demands Seeing reality for what it is. You must know how to distinguish fantasies from reality so as not to let your imagination play tricks on you.

58

Objective observation viewed through the "I Am" perspective is paradoxical in that the absolute is immanent in the relative. I observe the world through the eyes of the Living God so I can live in a willfully conscious way. To learn to observe the world as it is may require lengthy training, but when you live consciously you can claim to be truly alive. It is worth resisting the desensitization instituted by the manipulative plutocratic system and developing a vision of the world based on freedom and consciousness.

59

The thousands of hours I spent sketching people in parks and cafes taught me to See the world instead of merely looking at it. To draw the body and face of a person in public places requires efficiency, speed and subtlety. People move, they do not hold a pose long and they get nervous if they notice they are being observed. You must therefore look at them without fixing them. You learn to quickly glean the geometric structure of the model on which you can, given the time, add details and ultimately shadows and light. This technical exercise allowed me to develop the ability to fix in my memory a photographic image that sums up the essence of what I want to draw. I am able to see the world and synthesize its essence without losing myself in the details. The world is filled with signs and symbols that show us the right path, which tell us that we are living harmoniously or try to draw our attention to warn us about something.

The landscape perceived by the one who lives in a willfully conscious manner is all-encompassing—a vast perspective he offers himself from his exalted vantage point. For those living only at the first level, on the other hand, the world is poor and meaningless because they cannot give meaning to the information they are offered, even if it is abundant.

60

To be willfully conscious is to accept that you stand alone before the infinity of your consciousness. The vast luminous spaces stretch out as far as the eyes can see. The realization that these spaces are a part of you can be staggering.

61

In overcoming my nothingness joyfully, I send a clear signal to the world. I tell it that, despite the absurdity of doomed life, and by extension mine as well, there is every reason to rejoice, for a part of me will survive in spite of everything. Against all odds, I am getting used to the idea of immortality; I dedicate myself to it without taking into account the opinion of my contemporaries, for this state of Being has nothing to do with them.

62

There is nothing now for me but to maintain a permanent center of gravity inside myself that will survive me as a person. I pour all the strength of my intelligence into it and try to surround myself with individuals who, like me, are obsessed with this idea. I endeavor to keep this key word at the center of my consciousness: permanence. And the more I think about it the more I appreciate the solitude.

63

To live in a willfully conscious way means integrating your human nature on a higher plane without suppressing it. It consists in juxtaposing your person with your Being in order to have access to infinite knowledge, to infinite manifestation, while remaining in the world. With discernment, you can remain focused on the essential. I delight in my self by satisfying as many of its desires as possible, while remaining constantly aware of my divine nature. I have to be bold to assert that I am the Living God. But I don't give weight to the moral judgment of others, so that I can invest myself entirely in my own consciousness. Nor do I expect to be understood. I am content to Be with an intensity that will still radiate hundreds of years from now.

64

Joy is essential to living in a willfully conscious way. Being permanently happy is an absolute state where the individual is aware there is nothing to do to improve the world, perfect as it is at the moment when it is perceived. In this peaceful state it is possible to be willfully conscious because the self is not perturbed by insignificant details, which, though still perceived, no longer monopolize the individual to the point of distracting him from the essential. Problems that seem terribly urgent to the majority are greeted with an indifferent shrug. It is not that the willfully conscious being has no compassion, but rather that the perspective he has of the world is so vast that for him it is clear that all answers are contained in the questions.

65

Being lastingly joyful facilitates clarity because unnecessary worries are eliminated. It is sometimes good and healthy to worry about important things, but the one who has learned to live in a willfully conscious way has trained himself to quickly regain surface calm without ever losing his profound serenity. The anchor he has cast grounds him firmly in his Being. Even if his dinghy pitches dangerously, the dominant aspect of what he is remains seated on the fine soft sand of the depths where no tide can disturb it.

66

When I look at my life in its entirety, I cannot help but notice the lengths I went to maintain the state of an attentive observer. I cannot say I always lived in the willfully conscious way I do now, but it's clear that everything in my personality lead me inexorably towards becoming a willfully conscious being. My artistic nature means I have always been a keen observer of the world. I often preferred not to take part in it so as to have the joy of observing it. I analyzed it, this world; I studied it under the microscope before deciding to participate in it. It is only now that I really feel part of it. I did not enter the job market until I was thirty-five years old because I saw no interest in it other than to satisfy the need for money, which I had found a way to do without having to work, anyway. But at one point I realized that to live my human life to the fullest, I would have to take part as much as possible in the customs of my time. This has led me to meet extraordinary people with whom I forged bonds of friendship. Like a yogi, one can observe the world and renounce it, or one can choose to participate in it consciously, like a bhogi, using the experience to make firm the awakened state. By constantly running up against the limits of this world and the people who constitute it, I reinforce my ability to keep my attention fixed on the essential. This is what I call living in a willfully conscious way.

67

Those who already have a good sense of observation already possess an essential quality that, if developed assiduously, can help them develop the capacity to live in a willfully conscious way. They must, of course, be totally obsessed with this desire, that nothing and no one can distract them from it. Only then can they make use of this aptitude to lead them to enlightenment... something that is practically impossible to attain on this planet.

68

I'm an artist right down to my fingertips, and it has made me a keen observer of the world. I remember how obsessed I was with this when I moved to Montreal and started my adult life. I spent my days filling my notebooks with sketches and I used the best ones to create giant drawings that I pasted on my walls. I also incorporated them in my comics by surrendering myself to all the fantasies that my unbridled imagination offered me. I had the sincere impression that I was finally Seeing the world as it is. I no longer had to toe the line at school and I promised myself I would attain freedom at all costs. I dare say that I succeeded because today a sense of freedom fills me. I looked at the world with such intensity that I captured its essence. I applied all my talents to express it: drawing, music, poetry and writing. I believe I captured this essence in my art. And little by little, as I awoke spiritually, I applied this artistic penchant to higher planes. Today I truly have the sense that I look at the world through the eyes of the Living God.

69

The willfully conscious life means knowing how to observe the world carefully in order to remain unflinchingly focused on the essential. It can be practiced through observational drawing because it requires entering a state that closely resembles that of the Observer. Like the Buddha who fixes his inner gaze on what is most subtle in him, the artist learns through the practice of his art to detect the slightest subtlety of form, color and texture in order to render it truthfully in his art. It is not easy for one who lacks patience. For one with self-control, though, the rewards come quickly. When he draws from his imagination, his characters are portrayed better, his landscapes are more balanced and the perspective is right. Should he explore abstract art, his lines and colors will be in perfect harmony, and the work will be perfectly balanced as a whole even if at first glance it seems to be pure chaos. Few understand that to make abstract art it is first necessary to master figurative art. Likewise, to be a master of the absolute, you must first master the relative. To live in a willfully conscious manner you must accept your self and love it unconditionally, and from this sturdy foundation explore the absolute, carefree.

70

There are so few sentient beings living in a willfully conscious manner on this planet that it is clear that I can only speak about my personal experience. My art played a catalytic role in activating the immutable in me. Everything happened smoothly, effortlessly. I have always been very inspired and this inspiration bestows on me an astonishing velocity. I let myself be carried by this wave which, more often than not, brings me to where I need to be. When I am asked for advice about conscious life, I always answer, "Follow your bliss." This is what I have always done, and it has taken me to the very heart of my self. My experience has confirmed what I knew intuitively and what I understood intellectually: it is by following my natural predisposition that I have the best chance of being happy, because only in doing so do I sate my desires. I bring to fruition every project I undertake and then move on to something else without a second thought. In that moment I am satisfied with my life. I know I have done all that is humanly possible to be in harmony with what I have set out to be in this life. This makes me a free being, and therefore very dangerous.

71

It is common today to say that we are all equal, that we all have a soul and a spirit. Personally, I don't believe it. This levelling down is an insult to intelligence and diametrically opposed to individuation, which is the foundational principle of conscious life. A willfully conscious individual does not wonder what others think. Morality polices thought and its aim is to homogenize us in order to prevent us from accessing consciousness, freedom and happiness. I cannot compare myself to anyone else because I am unique. All resemblance is only superficial and to dwell on it is the purview of the unconscious masses. By drawing inspiration directly from the source of my Being, I have access to infinite knowledge. The source is in me and I nurture it consciously so that, in turn, it nourishes me with the absolute that I so need to keep my balance. I am equal to no one. Those who try to put me in a mold to better understand me miss the point. I am an exception because I have nothing left to lose. In conscious life, death is no longer an option. I want to be irreducible, ungovernable and violently singular.

72

In terms of intelligence, talent and potential, we are all very different, and that very difference can enable us to assert our individuality. Since enlightenment happens through the self, it is impossible for one who forgets his self constantly to awaken. One must definitely be an immoralist in order to live in a willfully conscious way. Morality is mediocre, ordinary and tasteless, whereas ethics are personal, original and permanent. Only the one who has developed a personal set of ethics can, and dares, think for himself. This is unfortunately not the norm on this planet, but from where I stand now, it does not matter anymore. Conformity makes me sick. The mass of people who unquestioningly accept the programming of the manipulative plutocratic system are dead and have not yet begun to act willfully. Without necessarily believing myself superior to all those who are asleep, I know that I am radically different from them at the level of my essence. And yet, at the level of my Being, I am not separate from them and I incorporate them into the immensity of what I Am. Conscious life is violently repressed on this planet. He who pursues it will find himself constrained and opposed from all sides. But if he follows his Being without hesitation, he will eventually place himself under the law of exception. So few people get this far that it is more realistic to say that it is impossible to attain on Earth. At least like this all hope is quashed.

73

Utmost despair leads inexorably towards enlightenment. Only one who has lost all hope lives in the here and now. He has given up trying to improve himself because he understands that the world is perfect. He can thus truly appreciate the present moment, taste it shamelessly, because for him, only the primordial ever-present exists. I am talking here about a blissful despair that has nothing to do with depression. I know despair, for in my heart I have stopped hoping. I am established in paradise here and now and I intend to stay there.

74

Last night I saw flashes of white light in a dream. White light is the ultimate experience, and the fact that I experienced it, even briefly, demonstrates to me that writing a book such as this can only enhance this state which defines me. I feel a sublime clarity in me. I sense telepathically those who think of me, in real time. I also see that everything in my life has its place, that nothing is left to chance. And because I feel such harmony I am able to experience this white light which emanates from deep inside me. I feel it in every pore of my skin. I am willfully conscious. I stand tall even though hardly anyone sees me for what I Am. The effort I put forth to live in a willfully conscious manner shaped in me a permanent center of gravity. It is marvelous, except that hardly anybody understands it. My clients are ignorant of the fact that they are dealing with a saint. Most of the time, it does not bother me. I play the game... because I must. But one day I will explode in the face of the world.

75

Being willfully conscious implies a risk factor the majority of humans are not willing to accept. The truth is often brutal and few seek it out on this planet. And yet, conscious life is the best option. I do not own anything; no car, no house, no RRSP. I will not have children. I do not expose my flank to those who would hurt me. I gamble everything on my creative work. The concept of "taking a vacation" seems absurd to me. When I have money, I invest it in my art. There is so much to do because I am consecrated, and yet everything happens inside me. I work in the realm of the permanent. All these people who spend their money on two-week trips to an exotic country seem ridiculous to me. They'd be better off investing in my art. They would then learn the true meaning of the word "vacation."

76

The willfully conscious individual generally faces a complete lack of understanding from his contemporaries. In order to survive the awakening he must dissociate himself from the mass of the unconscious who waste their time working like beasts of burden for a few mouthfuls of bread. I lived a long time without working and I'm doing very well. Work uses one up and distracts from Being. To think, you must have time. He who devotes himself to consciousness knows this well and minimizes his ambitions to ensure they do not distract him from what is permanent. It is this part of me that I cherish. I cannot get enough of it because it is through it that I enter the absolute even though I am still in the relative.

77

The willfully conscious individual has mastered his fears... not that fear is no longer there, or that he no longer observes it inside, but rather that it no longer has the power to disturb him. He who is frightened by the unknown is still controlled by his animal nature. His hormones distract him from where he should be. I still feel fear sometimes, but I do not let it dominate me. I do not scamper away like a rabbit; I listen to my Being instead. I seek out the signs, the suggestions from the invisible. I allow myself to think and ultimately I win out, even if at the moment everything seems lost. Every problem contains its own solution. And if I panic and let adrenaline make me deaf, I will miss the solution, in all its simplicity, which lies at the very heart of the problem.

78

I have unleashed an inexhaustible source of energy in me and I let it grow. It is my Being that I freed, like a sleeping God. I feel carried by this source that springs from me and manifests in the world. Its vitality astounds me. I long felt the existence in me of an entire universe that sparkled with vitality, but today I feel differently. When I experienced the realization that the universe is simultaneously in me and that I am the universe, I crystallized my permanent center of gravity. One cannot forget such an experience. It is the most tangible teaching of non-duality. Only then did I understand the true meaning of Yin and Yang. The source springs from me and at the same time I am this very infinite source of light. This realization makes me fully conscious that I am not just my self. It is impossible for me to feel limited because I carry the absolute in me. Through this light I live in permanent clarity.

79

By being willfully conscious, I am better able to seize the beneficial opportunities that come to me, and avoid those that are not. It is as if a radar keeps me constantly informed of the intentions of those around me and of events that could have an impact on my life. For me, it is especially clear thanks to the attention I pay to my dreams. I often guess in advance what a person intends to do. At their clearest, the signs are so easy to interpret that I cannot but notice how important things are always announced to me. I see one prepare to hurt me and another intensely desiring me. I don't usually have to wait long before my intuition is confirmed. I find this very gratifying. I feel that if I remain attentive, I will never be caught unawares.

I think well of my self. I understand that my person is what matters most because through it I perceive the world. It is therefore by loving it out of all proportion, by taking care of it and by nurturing it intelligently that I place myself in the best position to appreciate the willfully conscious life. I prefer myself over anyone. If the thought of doing something does not excite me, it is unlikely that I will do it because I have dedicated myself to thinking everything through ahead of time. I usually arrive early to my appointments in order to get a feel for a place and give myself time to harmonize with it before others arrive. By thinking of everything ahead of time, I am less likely to be taken advantage of. I do not get involved in a relationship unless I feel that the other person will respect my freedom.

81

To think well of yourself means knowing how to truly enjoy yourself. I deliberately add the word "truly" because I have noticed that most people have a preconceived idea of what might make them happy, but don't give themselves what they really want. How many people spend extraordinary amounts of money on trips, while deep down, their most cherished desire is simply to write a book or carry out a project that is close to their heart? They live friendly or loving relationships with people who do not truly care for them. They give up their own dreams to please others. At the end of their lives, these people are dissatisfied. Every day I make sure I'm on the right track... my track. I, too, must now work to earn money. I do not really have a choice, but fundamentally, I have not yet compromised. I organized myself to be able to work from home because that's where I feel the best and I'm the most productive. If I get tired, I take a nap and continue my work when I have the energy. It seems so simple and yet I know few who do as I do. They can talk about it, find the idea enticing, but when it comes time to take action, they will opt for a full-time company job that will force them to work on a fixed schedule. These people have clearly forgotten what is essential.

82

To live in a willfully conscious manner on this planet is no small task. Humans are, as a whole, too ignorant to even grasp this concept. It makes things complicated at times, which is why I choose the most accurate words to describe my state of being and my actions.

83

He who lives in a willfully conscious manner has a very intense vibration, which can make others feel uncomfortable or even upset. You have to see it to believe it. By dint of disconcerting people, I learned to stay in my center and leave it as rarely as possible. I learned to let them come to me. To seduce means to attract, not invade. I therefore arrange, whenever possible, to invite people to my house; seldom will I go to parties if I feel I will be the only one there consciously alive. This is for my own safety... but especially for that of others.

84

To live intensely means to en-light-en, not burn to the ground. Today, many people believe themselves to be very intense. They work like crazy, spending more hours in front of their computer screen than with their friends and family. They busy themselves with futile things under the pretext of making money. I have nothing against this idea, but for me it's not what I do, but how I do it. I have a quiet intensity; my nature is calm and peaceful. I give the impression of moving slowly... but I get where I want to go. My action is constant because it is grounded in permanence. I am productive without wasting energy. Thus, I do not burn myself out by wanting to do everything at once. I keep repeating this wise thought to myself: "A little every day."

85

Living intensely, in an intelligent manner, means allocating your attention to your entire Being in an integral way. I am not like those workaholics who think only of working and forget to take care of their physical body, their family and their emotional life. I admit that I tend to be compulsive and radical in my desires, but over time, I realized that an integral practice was necessary for me to remain happy and satisfied with my life. What good is it to succeed in business, to be very rich, if it leaves me no time to dedicate myself to my art, to women and to make my body strong and healthy? So I learned to stay balanced, to devote a little time each day to everything I care about. I drew up a map of all the levels of my self: body, heart, soul and mind and their interrelation with personal, social, community, cosmic aspects. In diversifying myself in this way, I ensure living life on this plane in a conscious way. Intensity has to be educated through intelligence to be fruitful; otherwise something monstrous may spring forth from it.

86

To live intensely implies enjoying everything to the maximum. I am very sensitive to beauty; as soon as I detect it somewhere I delight in it. There is always a little bit of beauty around me; I know how to find it and take the time to admire it because I am an inveterate man of pleasure. I educated my senses so they could capture the invisible. The world gives me every reason to believe that I have reached a high level of sensitivity. This is reflected in my artwork, though I do not feel like I have worked that hard. My creativity is constant and I do not lack inspiration. By living in a willfully conscious manner, I am intense because I am centered. I understand that I am energy, and that it renews itself constantly if I expend it.

87

To live in a willfully conscious way means being open to the impossible each and every moment.

What normal people define as the world is far from what my own perception leads me to believe it is. It is no longer possible for me to find external models, but it doesn't bother me; I'm a prolific creator. Inventing worlds is natural to me. My experience as a cartoonist has shown me that nothing is impossible. I remain convinced that this is so at the most subtle levels of reality.

88

Conscious life begets the impossible. Living in consciousness implies feeling the paradox of the world deep within you. In a world limited by time and space, it is easier to feel the unlimited aspect of consciousness; limits allow you to touch the infinite. To be prisoner in a physical body that has a beginning and therefore an end is but a short interlude. The wisest use it as an opportunity to create a permanent center of gravity. My subtle body, for example—my dream body—is immensely vaster and more mature than my self. By getting used to staying in my center of gravity, I will continue to think after the death of my Body-for-Others (the one that others perceive; the one they imagine to be me), a death that for all intents and purposes does not concern me. It is my Body-as-Being-for-Itself (my own body, the one I represent to myself) that I am concerned about because it is this one that permits me to enter eternal life. To live in a willfully conscious way is to stop worrying about the passing of time and to remain centered on the here and now. There indeed exists a pure state devoid of all duality and it is immanent to time and space.

89

I don't ask myself whether something is impossible. In fact, I erased the word "impossible" from my vocabulary a long time ago. A somewhat too rational person once asked me to climb a building and throw myself off to prove that I am immortal. I replied that I did not feel the need to demonstrate my point, least of all in such a crude manner. If I can conceive of something, if I can picture it, manifesting it is only a small step away. At the physical level, there are many limitations that must be respected. At subtle levels most of these limitations disappear. Flying then becomes possible, as much as being a woman or an animal. When I finally cross over to the absolute everything becomes possible because it contains infinite possibilities. That's what matters to me.

90

I am the master of the impossible because my imagination tolerates no limit. This plays against me sometimes and that is why I have been striving for several years to put my folly in check. I don't want to slow it down or control it, but more than anything I don't want its uncontained power to hurt me. Genius is like that—it's an overflow that pours out non-stop without deference to what is useful. My unbridled imagination often goes far beyond the situations that present themselves to me. This visionary aspect serves me well in my creative work because I am at home there, but when it comes to interacting with others or with the world, it gets complicated. The world plods along at its own speed and mine is obviously too fast and sometimes puts me in precarious situations where no one can understand me. But I'm still standing, despite evidence to the contrary, confident in myself and my ability to reinvent myself whenever I need to because I have understood the phrase: "Be the change you want to see in the world."

91

To stand erect in a state of awakening, despite evidence that this state is of no interest in this world, can be disconcerting. I tell myself that I have traveled all this way to attain enlightenment and now that I have reached it, I have nothing more to do with this world. I have integrated it at a deeper level and this is what is most difficult to explain. To live in a willfully conscious way seems to me to be the ultimate goal, and yet I see so few references to this state of being in everyday life, in the media and in the concerns of my contemporaries that it leaves me somewhat perplexed. I sometimes observe anger pass through my self. I try not to identify with it, but sometimes it is impossible to avoid and I get sick. Deep down, though, I know that my self is only a tiny part of what I Am. It may well get sick but it does not affect the peace that I feel in the depths of my Being. In spite of everything, I stand erect, even if I am shoved by a crude oaf or someone insults my intelligence through his actions. I turn to my creative work and note everything in my journal, knowing that one day the truth will erupt and my actions and my thoughts will be recognized for their true worth.

While others are on their knees, the one who
lives in a willfully conscious way stands straight
and tall. And yet, the paradox is that, most of
the time, he goes unnoticed. The greatest realized masters rarely have more than a dozen
followers. That is their strength. Their energy
is extremely concentrated and the privileged
few who receive their teachings have the time
to integrate what they receive. It is enough to
observe the life of Socrates, Pythagoras, Jesus,
Buddha or Nisargadatta Maharaj to realize the
truth of this. The more people around a teacher, the more diluted his teachings and the
less likely he is to last. I met a master, and I go
to his house every Saturday to attend his phi-
losophical discussions. Most of the time there
are two to four people in attendance. And yet,
he is one of the greatest geniuses of philosophy.
It's clear to me that the greatest of masters is
inevitably invisible to the majority; this is what
gives him his strength. By ceasing to identify
with my self, I lost my ambitions.

93

He who lives in a willfully conscious manner is
not afraid of the truth, even though he knows it
can be dangerous. The people who enter my life
wanting to ply their insanity on me grow disen-
chanted quickly. I desire the truth so much. I
understand why they think I'm crazy but I can
show that, in fact, they are the ones who are. I
prefer, however, to approach the subject univer-
sally in my books. I'm not afraid of the truth. I

experienced completely unhinged states during psychedelic experiments. I never identified with this madness, though. It is not a part of my essence but rather that of the world in which I live. If I were truly mad, I would accept this madness as reality and do my best to live my life. But by situating myself in the truth, I see myself in my perfection. I'm not afraid of my folly.

94

Those who see me as God's fool, like St. Francis of Assisi or Socrates, are right. They have perceived my true nature, and by acknowledging it to me, they validate the fact that they are also that. Because like knows like, the one who lives in a willfully conscious way is unrecognizable to those who have not willed that state in themselves.

95

The willfully conscious man is an adult. The level of maturity I have attained over the last few years sometimes astounds me. It is difficult for me to relate to people who seem to have no interest in rising above their warm-blooded animal nature. This is especially noticeable in relationships. As soon as two humans fall in love, their IQ seems to instantly fall to that of adolescents. Why this happens is beyond me because I would rather establish a real relationship with adults than take care of a nursery. He who lives in a willfully conscious way loves truth above anything, while the majority seems more comfortable creating an illusion that has nothing to do with truth. Thus, after several years of living together, lovers become strangers to one another because they cannot express their true nature. The sage can look the truth in the face and he will prefer it to the alternative even if it causes pain, because it is the only possible option for a conscious life.

96

Conscious life is not fashionable today. The manipulative plutocratic system desensitizes us as soon as it can to take away the little chance we have of awakening in this world. I struggled doggedly to get away from the collective anesthesia. I had to work with psychedelics for want of meeting a teacher worthy of the name. I was already thirty-two when my conscious life began. Had my educators supported such a state in me from childhood, I would already have been familiar with it. Instead, I traveled through a world hostile to consciousness, without teachers and left to my own devices. I have come to understand that awakening is an unnatural act and that life has no interest in a man awakening. Nature runs headlong towards its doom; it is in constant decline towards chaos, whereas the conscious man has established permanence in himself. He has understood that life is a bad trick that consciousness plays on itself. He resists passively. He has understood that beyond the world of representations there is consciousness—infinite and absolute. That is what we should teach children instead of mathematics and science. They have plenty of time to study these subjects later, of their own accord, if they so desire. At least in this way they would not lose touch with their consciousness and lose the habit of paying attention to it.

97

It is through my creative work that I can best realize this state. For me, writing carries a great deal of responsibility. That's why I waited to be clear to begin expressing my ideas in writing. I am conscious that when I formulate my ideas, I send them out into the world. In representing them to myself, they have an effect. Even though my books have yet to be published on a large scale, I feel that my ideas already have an impact on the world. I do not just write. I constantly imagine other ways of thinking about conscious life: I stick phrases on the walls, I create radio and television programs, I put in place an organization centered on the teaching of conscious life and much more. Everything brings me back to the fundamental idea of my life: live in a willfully conscious way.

98

I find it impossible to take seriously those who live their lives mechanically without ever dreaming that they could, once and for all, free themselves from the infernal cycle of reincarnations. I do not accept that others, or even this world, impose on me their karma. Reincarnation is the unbreakable chain that reduces man to the status of a slave. Just like an elephant accustomed to being shackled by a chain that is then replaced by a cord that it could easily break, man is enslaved by the idea that he has karma or that he has to expiate an original sin. If there is an original sin, it has nothing to do with what I Am. Woe to the person who speaks to me of my karma when I am facing trying moments, because I might just joyfully bring the hammer down on the ignoramus who dared use such senseless words. If I get sick or if a difficult experience befalls me, it is the result of my thoughts at the time, in the here and now.

99

Karma emanates from the general law. It fosters guilt in man and the acceptance of the worst injustices. I do not have karma. I am not here to purify myself, but to be. I do not evolve, I am evolved. The "I Am" is stronger than anything because it is beyond time and space. Karma implies the concept of reincarnation, an infernal wheel that deserves to be shattered on the very head of those who teach it. I propose to establish myself vertically to the world instead of pinballing indefinitely on the horizontal. To do that seems much more intelligent to me, because we're taught from childhood that we are sinners and that we are not worthy of holding the title of God. I often amuse myself by saying that I am the Living God. I like to see the stupor on people's faces. I hear them thinking to themselves, «How dare he?" I can see clearly that they never thought of themselves as God. And even if it were not true, by dint of thinking about it, it is more likely to manifest than by believing that it takes multiple reincarnations to attain the right to be God. I agree with the idea that I have several lives, but mine are not successive, they are simultaneous. I therefore endeavor to enable here and now the infinite number of possible lives in which "I Am" including this one, so that at the time of death of my body-for-others I will not be fooled. It is knowing that I am "joy-energy-freedom-consciousness" that I will leave this world, and not with thoughts of coming back to expiate or finish something.

100

To live in a willfully conscious way, you must have the strength to refocus as soon as you feel yourself moving away from your Being. There is no shortage of decentering challenges in this world, but he who has succeeded in crystallizing a permanent center of gravity in himself has no difficulty in remaining centered. This may seem like a paradox, but moments that decenter me allow me to refocus even more. It has become second nature to me to not forget myself, to prefer myself over anyone. I no longer wait for the approbation of others to give myself the right to do what I love. I realize that at my age, most people have given up on enlightenment because it would require a superhuman effort to start over. I have made it clear for a long time that I am determined to follow only my own desires, even if it displeases others and compels me to travel this road alone. By keeping the rudder steady, I realize that I have become a source of inspiration to those who love me. They understand that I represent permanence, that my uniqueness makes me a universal being.

101

It takes refined discrimination to distinguish centeredness from selfishness. Animals generally do not have this difficulty; they see the world in all its purity. Since I no longer identify with my self, it is very difficult for me to admit that I can be selfish. I think well of myself and of my friends, even if they do not know how to benefit from it. If I pull the covers to my side of the bed, it is because my Being inspires me to do it and I don't question it. If someone else pulls on them with equal strength, then I will not fight and I will leave them some. The one who does not know how to live in infinite abundance cannot become the Living God. Don't be a doctor to the incurable. The sufferers who complain incessantly are selfish. They do not know how to give themselves the essential and therefore cannot redistribute it intelligently. This is why I invest all of the energy of despair into pulling the covers to my side as much as possible to benefit the friends of my essence.

102

My school of conscious life is inspired by the altered states of consciousness I experienced a few years ago through psychedelics. I dove into the deep end and had to read compulsively to figure out what was happening to me. Luckily, I wasn't working then and had plenty of time to think. I gave myself the task to enter fully into the absolute because I no longer felt I had to journey for several years to get there. So I refused to accept there were steps to follow, telling myself that what mattered most was being at the pinnacle of myself, here and now. I sensed that once established in the heart of the absolute, I would be intelligent enough to find a way to integrate it into the relative. I believe I succeeded. I am a happy man, satisfied, and more than anything, I feel free. The psychedelics helped me become familiar with freedom by giving me access to fantastic experiences. Thus I experienced consciousness concretely, devoid of the self, without object, monist.

103

Psychedelics were the catalyst of my conscious life. I don't know what I was looking for, but I never imagined finding this. The awakened state was unintelligible to me before, but thanks to psychedelics, I managed to represent it to myself, and more than anything, experience it. Therein lies the essence of their power to awaken. You can study the awakened state as much as you want but rational understanding has no value without the concrete experience. It is only then that everything starts making sense. Intellectual understanding serves as a foundation for capturing this state and making it manifest on the physical level. To live in today's society in a full and satisfying way, it is important to be able to explain to myself what I Am. For me as an intellectual, this is essential. I cannot count on others to understand the state of sanctity; it is too much to ask of them.

104

Consciousness is a realm of manifestation; the awakened one realizes that this space is him into infinity. I had a surprising experience while on LSD. I suddenly saw myself from behind looking at myself into infinity. An infinite chain of "Is" was looking at the back of the "I" ahead of him, evoking fractals. I suddenly realized what was happening, and when I laughed, I turned around. All the "Is" turned towards me, but since I was watching the scene, I realized that there was still an observer who saw the scene without turning; otherwise I would have turned my head to look behind me. This experience gave me first-hand knowledge of the concept of the Observer. I realized then that consciousness is a realm of manifestation and that the world is but a representation within it. Consciousness is immutable; it is the sum of all that exists and at the same time it exceeds this sum by encompassing it in the absolute. I understood that I am this immutable Observer and that the world moves within me without it being necessary for me to act.

105

Since consciousness is a realm of manifestation where I offer myself to perceive the world, living in a willfully conscious manner implies a certain level of detachment. I feel part of this world and yet I am only its observer. This paradox of reality must be integrated so as not to go mad with this insane equation. Few seem to have understood the second level of the Yin

Yang symbol. The majority seems to believe that it represents the balance of opposites, or that in the light there is always a little darkness and in the dark a little light. But for me it represents the unity of reality, which is at a superior level and accommodates opposites by considering them aspects of reality that are integrated in non-duality. But the rational human mind has great difficulty grasping this. Everything in our world encourages us to believe that duality alone exists. But with training, we can dislocate the mind to get it to accept a proposition whose two parts seem to be logically opposed. Yin Yang is the integration of duality into the homogeneous whole of monism. This is impossible to understand unless the paradox is integrated at a superior level. I once had an experience where I suddenly realized that the universe is in me and that at the same time I am this universe. I was in a state of altered consciousness where my dislocated mind could accept this. This state resembled that of the dream in which the most improbable things are accepted without problem. My mind did not close again following this experience. It remained open and from that moment on I could really understand the meaning of the absolute, which can lie at the very core of the relative without diminishing its essential quality.

106

The mystical experiences I had between the ages of twenty-eight and thirty-two gradually opened me to the invisible. I had to die to my old life and switch on my permanent center of gravity at a subtle level in order to be reborn. This second birth is that of consciousness. If the first is rather crude and difficult due to the fact that we are manifesting ourselves in a physical body, which tends to make us forget our true nature, the second is liberation from this cage of suffering and limitation which is the self. Does not the caterpillar become a butterfly? At first glance, they seem to have nothing in common and yet against all probability one becomes the other. I feel light and free. I remember the despair that preceded my liberation, how stifled and weighed down I felt by the constraints of the world. And then I found my way to the light, to finally understand and accept that this light is me.

107

Because I understand I am this realm of manifestation, I am much more cognizant of what I manifest within it. To live consciously is to be absolutely convinced that one is not separate from anything, and that one's intentions, thoughts and emotions become integral to this space as soon as they are emitted. It is therefore injurious to get indiscriminately angry or to brood needlessly because it impacts the world directly. I'm not saying you should never get angry. It is sometimes necessary to stir up action, but this anger should not come from the self but from Being. Only then will it be like a hurricane whose role is to rebalance the whole. There is the concept of "holy wrath." Jesus, for example, when he cursed the Pharisees or when he berated the merchants who used the temple as a place of business, did what his Being dictated to him. This is healthy and quite in the order of things. Today's dominant religions have led people to believe that a saint is always gentle as a lamb, which in fact is not the case. A saint is moved to anger by his Being, not by his self. I toss into the trash the castrated and sanitized version of the saint to replace it with that of the Greek gods, who, from high atop their kingdom, observed humans and punished them or made love to them when it was deemed necessary.

108

The Living God does not have to renounce his human nature. It would be absurd to take the trouble to be born into a child's body and undergo the difficult transition into adulthood, only to renounce it immediately like Jesus Christ. Having integrated the paradox, I can move from one to the other effortlessly. I have juxtaposed my self to my Being: at times I Am more than I think and at other times I think more than I Am. I am a Bhogi rather than a Yogi. That is to say, I do not give up anything. I want to refill, not renounce. I feel sated with everything. That satisfies me immensely. I especially love the small details of my daily life: my little cat who greets me when I wake up, or when I open my computer to check my e-mails that will determine the work to be done that day. I enjoy coffee in the afternoon and conversations with the women I meet to practice Spanish. It's no secret; I'm very comfortable at home. I don't even want to hear about travelling; the very idea of leaving Montreal irritates me. It is thanks to these boundaries I have drawn, as simple as they are, that I can devote myself totally to my art and women, my two favorite indulgences. This base-level routine allows me to lift my thoughts to their highest in order to see the world through the eyes of the Living God, without forgetting that enlightenment occurs through the self, and that if I neglect it, it will be more difficult for me to perceive the absolute in me.

109

Bringing the absolute back into the relative is a daunting challenge. To feel like one is the Living God is not difficult as such; what is demanding is to feel like this in a world polarized between the belief in a transcendent God, therefore external and superior, and atheism. It requires a great deal of flexibility and intelligence to overcome this preponderant two-headed majority and make oneself God. Investing time in Being is the only path to enlightenment. We do not ask for permission to awaken, it would be refused outright by the general law. No! To live in a willfully conscious way, one must be ready to do anything. Some are ready to do anything to succeed socially or financially, but when it comes time to get down to serious matters—to get free once and for all—suddenly the bravest back away, tail between their legs. I know the primordial idea of my life and I am ready to do anything to keep it alive and well. Herein lies the challenge: to bring this fundamental idea, which is an insuppressible desire for the absolute, back into this relative—even very relative—world of this early twenty-first century.

To live consciously is to feel like one is God every moment. But he who chooses to live like this in society must undergo rigorous training so as not to lose himself in the absolute which vibrates in him permanently. He cannot proclaim to the four winds that he is in such and such a crystalline state, that he is the conscious light. When I buy stamps or do my groceries, I go unnoticed. I try my best to look normal. I even take pleasure in it, which sometimes astonishes me. I do not need to wear a cassock to feel invested with spirit. I am rather discreet; it compensates for the outrageous things I write in my books, and which sooner or later will have the effect of a tsunami on the collective consciousness of my time.

111

It is possible for anyone to become a Christ. It is an accessible state, like that of the Buddha. Once attained, all that remains is to color it with your own unique self. The Psychedelic Master suits me: by creating my own myth, I answered my metaphysical questions. My questions now are more of a practical nature: How do I live in this state in a world where it is unintelligible? How do I keep my physical body healthy knowing that it also depends on the health of humanity as a whole? How can we fully live this Christ-like state without suffering the fate of Jesus? I have no more questions about the absolute, but rather how to bring it back and integrate it into the relative, without renouncing anything.

I am aware of having taken a path that few want to follow. I renounced having children to devote myself totally to my art. The biological family does not seem to me to be necessarily the true family, contrary to what the dominant majority believes today. But at the point where I am now, the opinion of others means little to me. I remember that my mother called me selfish when I got my vasectomy. This is a great illustration of the opinion of the dominant majority on procreation. But for me it is not my duty to make sure this race of sleeping bipeds is perpetuated eternally. Rather, I came to inspire those who want to escape from this eternal cycle. I cannot do it for them, but by living in a willfully conscious way, I can at least believe that I set a good example.

113

I like the phrase: "Be the change you want to see in the world." I understood long ago that I have no control over others, that if I want something to happen in my life, I have to do it myself. I continue writing books despite the disinterest of publishers to whom I send my manuscripts. And since I'm not one to wait for others, I publish them myself in small quantities. Like a squirrel, I have my cache and the day when I will be better known, I will reap the rewards of my hyperbolic confidence. Reflecting on the phrase above, I understand that I can demand the impossible of myself... and get it. This is not true of others, who show me repeatedly that they prefer to live like animals instead of making themselves God. I have come to no longer have expectations of the world. I found my happiness in myself, and the pleasure creation affords me is deeper than the discomfort of being an unknown artist. By changing myself, I create a slipstream and pull the world in my wake, whether it wants to or not. How can I demand that men cease to wage war if in me I am not totally at peace? So that's what I'm doing, with the belief that by doing that, I have a concrete impact on the world.

114

Changing myself seemed easy, but when I really set out to do it, I realized that in this world we are all linked to each other through an endless series of interconnected destinies. With time, I came to know myself well. But when I recognized I was inextricably linked to all the sleeping people inhabiting this planet, I was forced to ask myself whether it was worth changing. I came to the conclusion that I must do my best and then let my Being take care of the rest. When I trust myself, I find I can trust humanity. I don't care whether it survives or not because I am creative enough to imagine that elsewhere in the universe there are places where those who are established vertically can exist in peace. I feel like a visitor or an immigrant. The Earth seems so inhospitable compared to the perfect world where my essence resides. Humans are somewhat endearing to me... especially women. If you are not happy with this world, there isn't much you can do unless you realize that this world is in you, and only changing radically from within do you have a chance to influence it. And if, like Christ or the Buddha, you are able to create a permanent center of gravity, the change you desire may manifest itself well after your death. This is why it is more beneficial to change yourself than to wait for the outside world to change.

115

To change radically implies working on oneself, which goes against nature because it has no desire to see us escape it. The human body is a source of energy which feeds the universe without regard for individuality. The less one is individuated, the more one's nature is conventional, for it is a habit. From generation to generation, organisms reproduce the same habits without asking questions. But he who awakens is freed from this infernal cycle. He can be assured that as soon as the idea comes to liberate himself, everything will conspire to dissuade him. This is why it is more reasonable to say that it is impossible to awaken on this planet. Those who do are exceptions. The paradox is that for ordinary people in the West there is nothing to distinguish the awakened from the uninitiated. Of course, if someone dons a toga or goes naked like the sadhus of India, he will make others think he is different, but if Christ and the Buddha were alive in Montreal today, dressed like everyone else, they would probably go unnoticed. The Great Masters are not necessarily given to spectacle. If you change yourself radically, you should not expect to be recognized. This kind of change is far too subtle to be noticed by ordinary mortals. The important thing is to be aware of the change that you create in yourself and not to await the approval of others to live it. I am one of the few to notice it, but therein lies precisely the secret of this transformation—instead of waiting for the external world to change to mirror my inner perfection, I realize that by being conscious of my own perfection, I no longer expect anything from the outside world. Other people will always be only relative to my absolute.

116

Only those who live in a willfully conscious way can know happiness because it is established in the permanent. Happiness has nothing to do with the ups and downs of the ordinary man's everyday life; it is beyond this incessant to-and-fro. He who lives in consciousness has understood this. We all have difficult and painful moments; it is the lot of life on this plane. But how they are dealt with indicates the presence or absence of Being within a person. I have given myself a Being because it seems to me that the self with its limits is not suited for eternal life. It is naive to believe that when I die, Nicolas Lehoux will survive. Rather, I believe my myth will survive me. This part of me is vaster and less subject to the laws of physics. But still, beyond my myth, there is my Being, my "I Am." It alone is immortal because it exists beyond life itself. Without it, concepts of life and death have no meaning. Consciousness is a realm of manifestation. To identify with a specific part of this manifestation seems absurd to me. Everything that appears and disappears before my conscience can only be unreal.

117

I feel such happiness! It's incredible! The writing of this book makes me ecstatic. I am on the verge of having a fit of joy. I have so much energy! This is due to the intensification of my focus on the state I want to describe here, the state of one who, having freed himself, lives in a willfully conscious way.

118

The kingdom of dreams is the royal door to the world of consciousness. He who lives in a willfully conscious way pays particular attention to his dreams. He jots them down, studies them, interprets them and tries to give them meaning. Information that is difficult to perceive during the day becomes more evident at night because problems and routine activities are set aside for a few hours. I have often received signs about other people's feelings or situations to come. He who remembers his dreams shows that he is worthy of seeing the world through the eyes of the Living God.

119

The dream state is close to the conscious life. It is more concrete and real than the waking state. I find it strange that today the majority have come to think the opposite, whereas if you look at the history of mankind on this planet, there were times when the art of dreaming was the focus of daily concerns. It is still the same today in the least civilized cultures. They have maintained an intimate contact with psychic life. Therein lies wisdom, which consists of being attentive to the essential.

120

The main thing is to prioritize what is permanent. It is good to distract yourself occasionally and let your attention fall on objects that pass through your perception, but this should always serve to bring you back to permanence. Just as limits afford a better grasp of the unlimited, the intelligent man can enjoy the ephemeral pleasures of this world without forgetting that the absolute is the core of everything.

121

The essential is not very fashionable today. Nothing seems built to last: relationships, homes, jobs, objects, etc. The world around us is not conducive to meditation about the immutable. Through a long process of desensitization, which he calls evolution, modern man has cut himself off almost totally from his inner world. Therein lies the drama of humanity, which seems to be racing to its doom, like a pod of whales which, disrupted by ultrasound coming from our technologies, beaches itself on the shore. It is a very sad sight for one passing by at the moment. To see such noble animals die in such an absurd way is an image I would gladly do without, and yet it is this impression I have when I look at humans right now. They seem confused and disturbed by something they cannot understand. They run aground on shores while their natural habitat is the sea of consciousness. The natural habitat of Being is consciousness in intimate contact with eternity.

122

It is by being very attentive to the details of the invisible that I can let my Being grow. Because it is composed mostly of this fine contexture beyond waking perception, I am fortunate that from my childhood I had the good idea to express my inner world through my art. Since I began writing this book, I have been on the verge of having a fit of joy. My energy is so intense that I can almost touch it. Yesterday I organized a get-together at my home. It was a delightful success and in the evening, after making love with my partner, I began to see scintillating blue lights circling around me. I paid attention because I recognized the preliminary signs of a particular experience. The lights approached and I took in their subtle beauty. I went into ecstasy for a few seconds. This experience occurred because I was attentive to details and recognized their significance. To live in a willfully conscious way implies constantly scrutinizing the invisible in order to allow its Being to flourish.

123

The one who lives in a willfully conscious way is familiar with ecstasy because it is born of a feeling of harmony and deep peace. This relaxed and calm state allows me to feel the immanent beauty of the world; I can abandon myself to it and allow the source of light that resides in me to expand. I let it surface, so that by emanating from me, I can share it with the world.

124

It seems to me my Being grows a little whenever I start writing a new book. It expands slowly like the wings of a butterfly that has just emerged from its cocoon. I take care of my wings because they will carry me up into the sky. The ecstatic experience I experienced yesterday lets me know that this impression of a fit of joy is not only in my head. A few years ago, I reached ecstasy several times thanks to psychedelics, and now that I no longer consume them, I have no doubt as to the reality of the experience. My partner was glued to me, absorbing as much as possible the energy that emanated from me. I know what triggered this ecstasy; I felt deep harmony throughout the day as my elected family came to celebrate with me. This magical feeling of being in the right place at the right time and performing the right actions made this normally gentle light source overflow. It is evident that in paying closer attention than usual to the willfully conscious life, I induce in myself this state that I constantly think about in order to be able to express it clearly and intelligently. Each book is a new adventure, a pretext to integrate all my ideas into a coherent and singular whole.

125

I observe my life attentively; I let my inner gaze flow over the primordial ideas that make it so full. I realize that I have understood the abundance of the infinite. In my life, I have never wanted for anything. I have always had the right balance; when I need something it manifests itself in my life; when it is no longer necessary, I let it go without attachment. This makes room for the new. Too many people cling desperately to what no longer has a place in their lives. They are afraid of being without. It is precisely this fear that prevents them from accepting the new when it presents itself. I accept the unknown with a child-like openness because I realize that since matter does not exist, it is absurd to cling to the objects that surround me. This knowledge ensured the success of my high-dose psychedelic experiments. At those levels, clinging to illusory concepts can turn an experience into a nightmare. It is therefore better to simply remain open and let the flow of experience take its course. Just as water knows the way to the ocean, my self intuitively knows the path to my Being.

126

To live in a willfully conscious way has a light and audacious quality that modern man lacks. I function in the world but I am not fooled by it. I observe its transparency and beauty. I know intimately that it is mine. I know that the world I offer myself to perceive is in my image. I do not argue with the saviors of humanity who surround themselves with ugly, sick and handicapped people on the pretext of helping them because, unlike them, I am not a doctor to the incurable. Over time the vibration of others mixes with mine. It is therefore important for me to carefully select the people, places and situations that I engage daily. I am not suggesting never to have a thought for those who suffer, but rather to learn to think well of oneself first. The wise man minds his own business because he has understood that the world is in him and that it is enough for him to change himself for the world to inevitably follow suit. What I am addressing is not momentary thoughts but those we have been dragging around forever. They are the hardest to detect because we are so used to them. They have become invisible to us. I have important work ahead. If I let myself be diminished by those who have not grasped the meaning of the word consciousness, I do not honor this gift that is my own. By exploiting it to its fullest I can, in turn, offer humanity the essential to inspire it to be more beautiful and harmonious.

127

To live in a willfully conscious way requires long and methodical training. I base all my actions in permanence. I prioritize what is most likely to be permanent in my life. I have no control over others. That is why I choose to devote myself to my creative work and not invest myself in what could distract me from it. I develop my ideas over time and share them through my work so that those who want to come into my life know what to expect. I educated my senses to intuitively detect those who are only passing through. I give them no credence and do not try to attract their attention when they move away from me. I do the same with situations, clients and the place where I live. In fact, everything in me is focused on the idea of permanence because it alone leads me to eternal life. You cannot imagine yourself immortal if you have not taken the trouble during this physical life to train yourself for eternal life. Those who are adrift, without lasting relationships or a stable roof over their heads, are carried away from their center and await death to attain eternal life. Eternity is unintelligible to them. If a being does not have the sense of permanently residing in the infinite, if he does not cultivate it with methodical diligence, he has no chance of entering consciously into eternal life. Permanence is at the core of my preoccupations; I situate it at the very heart of my human life. It is by making myself God, here and now, that I can remain so. In that way, death no longer concerns me because I Am eternity.

128

I feel I have nothing left to lose. I have always felt that way, but now I can say it with full consciousness. Almost everyone has this feeling in adolescence, and for some it carries over into early adult life. But very few can honestly say they have nothing to lose at my age. I am thirty-seven, yet I still live on the edge of the abyss, without a safety net or material possessions. I have only one buoy; my art. As time progresses it becomes stronger and more prodigious. But I'm not afraid to start all over again if necessary. I am not afraid of dying; I have neither children nor house. My principal possessions are of the subtle order: I have a Being and ideas. None of this is quantifiable in dollars and cents. I am gradually developing a parallel economy, and when possible, I barter. For example, I exchanged the transcription of this book against the creation of a website. It gives me great joy to know that I am not duped by the system and that I am smart enough to get around its shenanigans and surpass myself. Money is a lure. I know that. And, of course, some is necessary to live in society, but we could develop so many alternatives if only the majority finally understood that those who govern us have no Being.

129

Truth is more important than my personal comfort. Nothing will distract me from it. This makes me dangerous to the general law because my transparency often reveals the murkiness of others. It makes them uncomfortable because they are not used to telling themselves the truth. Only the one who is permanent is likely to be true, and in today's world permanence is not fashionable. So I slow down little by little and strive to invest my human life with all the symbols of permanence that I can find. When I undertake something, whether a project or a relationship, it's always long-term. I know that in doing so I prepare myself intelligently for eternal life.

I do not want to follow fashions because they are transient. In fact, I want to be so unusual that I cannot be classified. On one hand, there will be all these passing fashions, these different styles people get tired of, and on the other, there will be me; timeless, unclassifiable and singular to the point of being universal. In Quebec, this year, there were big demonstrations in the streets and some people accused me being selfish because I did not participate. I understood that they were only a flash in the pan and what took place afterward showed me that I was right. As for me, I continued my reflective and creative work with a steadfastness that will serve in the long term. The protesters returned home and continue being dupes of the system. They will vote, buy on credit and study in an educational system that is sold out and trivializes them. That does not seem to me to be congruent. I prefer to appear like a loser today, because tomorrow the real agents of change will find in my books the shocking ideas they need to break the system and the programs that chain us to illusions. No! Really! Being fashionable is a waste of time. What excites me most is to be a classic.

131

There is a source of light in me that grows a little each day. I apply myself methodically to encourage it in its unfolding. Its stability is a source of genuine support. This light is more my self than myself. Since I have lit the fire of enlightenment in me, I must let it grow little by little so that it spreads out in the world. I must share it without strings attached, and especially without expecting anything in return. In any case, my Being knows how to reward me very well. One must be exceptionally well centered in this world to light this infinite source of energy. I know very few who have actuated their permanent center of gravity. Neither schools nor family teach this. So how can humans realize that the potential to be eternal resides in them? It is not surprising that the dominant majority still believes in a paradise after life or reincarnation. What ignorance! Paradise exists here and now if we bothered to open our eyes. And reincarnations, if placed in their true context, are only simultaneous unactuated lives. It is so unfortunate to see all these pilgrims endlessly seeking, whereas here and now they could decide to become God and actuate all of their lives simultaneously. What wealth! How disregarded it is! To give oneself eternal life is true wealth because it is nourished by the abundance of the infinite.

132

Living in a willfully conscious way implies appreciating the value of all the details that compose my life on this plane. I have recognized my perfection and I manifest it as much as I can. Perfection is found in the soundness of an act or a judgment, so I train myself to define my feelings clearly. Writing usually serves me well in this regard but if it does not, I seek out other means of expression. I am resourceful; I give myself new options constantly. I am fooled by neither my emotions, nor those of others. By constantly analyzing my feelings I can better position myself in relation to the world. I do not want to waste time in relationships that lead nowhere, whether in love, business, friendship or personal projects. I find myself a little cynical sometimes but by dint of the number fleeting relationships I have experienced I have learned to take my time in evaluating those who enter my world. It's not always easy to detect the fleeting ones as they lay it on thick from the start. Unfortunately, their profligacy is quickly exhausted and their departure is imminent. So I developed a personal approach to the enjoyment of the here and now. I expect nothing from others in the realm of the relative. I savor each moment as if it were my last, so that when the hour comes when jealousy and misunderstanding make those flee who, a few days before, predicted a long relationship, I welcome their departure with a shrug of the shoulders and continue to be attentive to the new which is likely just around the corner.

133

The ephemeral is the norm today, which brings about a shameful levelling downward as too few people seek that which could be of long-term benefit to the community as a whole. The one who lives in a willfully conscious manner is, on the contrary, completely open to what is eternal. Everything in his life is structured to last beyond human life. He seeks out contact with friends of a shared essence because they alone can ally themselves with him to manifest the immutable in this world. I will not have children because I do not base my family on blood relation and emotional ties, but on a sharing of Being, values and ideas. My elected family is comprised of those who vibrate like me. As for the others, I hope they also find their elected family. I do not like the idea of marriage and successive relationships. As much as possible I keep my distance from disturbing emotions. I prefer to live as an immortal by attaching myself only to what gives me the feeling of being eternal.

134

Many people enter my life only to leave a few months later. On the whole, I would rather they went their own way without noticing me. But I am afraid I must get used to it, because life on Earth is like that, apart from the few exceptions that delight and surprise me. This happens especially frequently in romantic relationships. My view of them is based on sharing and openness, love is not front and center. It is the feeling of being free and happy that takes precedence. The idea of being free is seductive in the beginning, and yet after a while, gregarious instincts surface and jealousy spoils everything. The fear of losing becomes unbearable. This emotion is a form of cancer that gnaws at the human heart. Most leave to return in their artificial conformity. They could open up and learn to be free, but they prefer to find partners they can put in a golden cage.

135

We cannot boast of living in consciousness if we still feel jealousy, because it cuts us off from it. The one who feels free and expansive is able to share without being afraid of losing. There are people who consider themselves generous when they give a penny to a beggar or help the poor children of a developing country, but they are unable to bless their partner if they want to start a romantic relationship with another person. A partner is not a possession; love should not blind us to the point of believing otherwise. Those who boast of their generosity often complain that the rich do not share their wealth... but do they share the vastly more important things like love? I apply myself to living simply. I don't need to possess anything or anyone. When one of my partners wants to begin a relationship with another man, I bless her and keep smiling.

136

Awakening is an unnatural act. It shatters the concept of life and death. The enlightened one is unintelligible to his contemporaries because they cannot conceive of such a state. Awakening renders the concept of karma, evolution and original sin obsolete. To live in a willfully conscious way is to resist with all one's might the masses of somnolent ones that seek at all costs to impose a morality they do not even apply to themselves. I do not grant the same importance to convention as the majority does. I accept solitude as a grace, which is why I have the strength to move at crosscurrent. I got a vasectomy so as not to be pulled in by my mammalian nature. I remove my body hair because I don't want to look like a monkey. Everything in my actions expresses this desire to resist this evil trick played on my self. Despite what the majority thinks, I am not a descendant of apes. Will they ever admit that matter does not exist and that nature is doomed?

137

He who lives in a willfully conscious way does not disobey himself. He knows how to distinguish between his true desires and society's deluded obligations. At twenty-three, I did not want to work, and I did not disobey myself. Social pressure was very strong but my desire to be free was even stronger, so I followed my natural predisposition. I focused on my self before surrendering anything to society. I have been confronted many times in my life with situations where my strongest impulses opposed what society wanted of me. To think well of others you must first think well of yourself. Too many people want to be useful and serve, but by doing so they forget that enlightenment passes through the person.

138

It is by thinking well of myself and putting myself first without compromise that I have been able to awaken from this collective dream that is the world. I inhabit it but I'm not fooled by it. Because I have escaped the box, I have a singular perspective on this world. I'm no longer a prisoner. I can enter and leave as I please. I have arrived. There is something irreducible in me. You cannot force me to follow the general law. My Being inspires me to resist with all my strength. I become dangerous if I am forced to do what I don't want to do. I have resources that amaze me. In case of need, I cry for help and my Being comes to my aid.

139

I can be wild. When I feel irritated by something, I make sure to let the source of the irritation know about it. The majority of people imagine saints to be soft and docile. It is certainly the image the Church has wanted to give of its saints, but "holy wrath" has its place. If my entire Being tells me to raise my voice and make a scene, then I do it. This doesn't happen often but some people have the gift to disrupt harmony with impunity. If my Being prompts me to intervene harshly, I do not disobey. They will think what they want, but when I lose patience it is because something is very wrong. Then I can be merciless, but just like an animal that sends out the message to be wary, my intentions are not bad. The leopard does not kill for pleasure but to feed itself, and if it gets angry, it is to defend its integrity, never for the mere pleasure or vice. I am also reminded of Krishna, who told Arjuna on the battlefield that since he was a warrior, he had to fight and kill, not with emotion or out of a desire for vengeance, but because that is what the situation called for, and that if he did not do it, it would bring even greater harm.

140

Living in consciousness is still a new phenomenon for me. I went all-out with psychedelics for nearly four years between the ages of twenty-eight and thirty-two. I violently gave myself a Being, and from that moment on, I had to live in a willfully conscious way to stay afloat under the mass of new information brought on by my new perceptions. My telepathic abilities increased tenfold. I must now live with this gift, which can trouble me as much as it can help me. I can hear some people think, and if my perceptions are not clear enough, I have dreams that clarify their intentions beyond a shadow of a doubt. Because I live in a willfully conscious manner, I have access to a great deal of information, which at first glance may not make any sense. So I learned to trust my intuitions even if sometimes the conclusions they lead me to seem totally crazy. I always end up proving to myself that my perceptions are indeed well-founded. I don't regret forcing open the doors of perception. This new way of life is infinitely more satisfactory. I remember how stifled I was in my 20s, how hard I tried to free myself of my rationalism. Now that I have succeeded, I know that there is no other way to live than in a willfully conscious manner.

141

I look at the world through the eyes of the Living God. I return again and again to this absolute position as watchful Observer of the world...from its creator's point of view. Every

day, through my work and my personal projects, I affirm myself as a creator. It is therefore
easy for me to identify myself with that part of
me that is the Living God. I only concern myself
for the immutable. Everything in my life takes
on that sacred quality that I cherish so much.
Each moment I feel the presence of the invisible
at the very core of the visible. This is what I
call Seeing the world with the eyes of the Living
God, which implies seeing beyond the representation of the world into the very heart of reality
where matter does not exist.

142

I reached an ecstatic state last week. It was
unexpected and absolutely gratifying. It
was born of a feeling of beauty and harmony
that had reached its climax. I pay homage to
consciousness through this book and my Being
repays me abundantly. Since I started writing
it, I have had many dreams of babies (who
represent my Being), and even dreams of white
light. Without a doubt, a powerful process has
been set in motion in me since I started writing
this book. One does not reach ecstasy simply
by snapping ones fingers. One must feel such
intense happiness that one is literally lifted
into bliss. I believe this state is the just reward
for one who lives in consciousness. Timothy
Leary suggested that ecstasy was nothing but
spiritual masturbation, and on his deathbed,
Ramakrishna admitted that he could have integrated himself better in the world instead of
spending his time in ecstasy. Those who live in
a willfully conscious way all face this dilemma
sooner or later.

143

I did not come to Earth to have children, enter in emotional relationships or consort with humans horizontally at all. Rather, I came here to help them establish themselves vertically to the world. I know that I did not evolve from the ape. I constitute the world here and now. The ideas of karma and original sin do not accord with what I Am. No matter how emphatically others try to impose them on me, they just don't stick; I live in the ever-present origin and conceive the world from this immanent center, not from a life line stretching between the past and the future. I Am timeless. I exist in all eras of the world because I Am beyond time, space and history.

144

Conscious life far surpasses spirituality, which is only one of its most subtle aspects. To live in a willfully conscious way, I must pay attention to the entirety of what I am. Too many people today imagine that enlightenment is only about spirituality, but there is a difference between spiritual awakening and the awakening of Being. Through my integral practice, I pay attention to all aspects of my self. Living in consciousness implies knowing that all aspects of my Being are part of the Great-All-that-I-Am and that if I privilege certain aspects to the detriment of others I will not feel balanced. This means that sometimes I have to moderate my compulsive desire to learn and create art in order to take time for my friends, lovers, phy-

sical body and community. Happiness results
from a subtle balance between all aspects of my
self in the world.

145

Consciousness is constitutive in the sense that
it constitutes the world that I give myself to perceive. Being a creator, it is easy to integrate this
idea into my daily life. The world around me is
in my image. It reflects back to me what I am,
like a mirror, with a precision that is at times
shocking. It is easy to see oneself as the creator
of one's reality when all is well, but when we
fall ill or misfortune befalls us it is more difficult to accept that we created the situation for
us to reflect on ourselves. I accept the most difficult tests because I do not react like a victim;
I do not blame others for my misfortunes and
I integrate those moments intelligently at the
most subtle level. I know that accusing others
in no way helps me gain any real understanding of a situation. So I constantly reflect on
myself in order to understand why I have created a particular situation that affects me. This
is the very core of the willfully conscious life,
which consists in feeling ourselves God in that
we constitute the world in consciousness to give
ourselves the pleasure of perceiving it.

146

Consciousness is a realm of manifestation
constituting my self and everything else. I
understood this by switching off my self through
a methodical process that led me to have a

conscious experience in which my self no longer existed. My consciousness does not need my self to be conscious. I am the impassive Observer of the world. It is the state of the Buddha that, through a long and tedious process, gave him peace and turned off his mind. Only then is it possible to see the world as it is, without prejudice or turmoil. Unlike the Buddha, I am not a monk; I renounce nothing. It is nevertheless good to experience this state, because it helps stop identification with one's person. Instead of permanently switching off my person, like a yogi, I juxtapose it to my Being in order to function harmoniously in the Western world in which I live.

147

Consciousness is constitutive. Whoever wants to know the absolute must go back to the very source of all that is constituted. This may seem impossible from the point of view of the rational mind, which is entangled in duality and cannot solve the enigma of the eye which sees itself. I decoded this enigma during a psychedelic experience in which I suddenly realized that I am the universe and that the universe is in me. At that point the nonlinear state I was in presented me with the opening necessary to perceive two aspects of reality at the same time. This is how I embraced the paradox of reality, in which the mind no longer rules and duality collapses in on itself, making it possible to perceive the world as a whole and where opposites no longer oppose but complement each other.

From there it is only a small step to apply it to oneself and at last feel full of the absolute.

148

The one who lives in a willfully conscious way is in a perpetual state of profound harmony. A soft glow that illumines life on Earth emanates from this inner peace. I feel that at the heart of what I Am there is a source of energy that grows every day. This feeling is so deep, I can hardly put it into words, but I must, because that allows me to realize it. Harmony never leaves me; everywhere I look, I see beauty. Not that I deny the ugliness that is present on this planet, but I willfully surround myself with what can uplift me. I am the creator of my reality; it is my intention that takes precedence over that of others. If I keep out of reach of those who want to do me harm, intentionally or otherwise, over time deep harmony settles in my life. I don't seek out problems. I am not actively interested in victims who could destabilize me through their repeated contact. I manifest this harmony willfully through intention. I resist the pleas of those who are not their own masters. They want to pull as many as they can into their wake. They ask us to work more, consume on credit, vote and buy insurance. I say, "No, thanks!" This is how I manage to feel in harmony with what I have set out to be.

149

There is a source of light in me that grows a little every day. It constantly surprises me, for my happiness intensifies with this expansion. Each day that passes shows me that it is always possible to stretch the boundaries of infinity. This happiness is a very powerful source of energy; I feel it passing through me. That is why it is essential for me to live in a willfully conscious way. This power that animates me could just as easily make me lose my mastery over my self. Indeed, every day I feel submerged a little deeper in an ocean of light that threatens at times to make me blind to the physical world. It's a bit like driving a car into the setting sun without sunglasses on. This causes many accidents. But the experienced driver will have thought of putting sunglasses on and pays attention to the smallest detail. To live in a willfully conscious way requires an acute attention to every detail because at any moment one can be engulfed by the immensity of Being.

150

I have established in me the equivalent of a well of light. I dug desperately for several years, devoting myself body and soul, without conceding anything. My despair was such that I had no choice but to continue without retracing a single step. Then suddenly I pierced the veil and found in myself a source of unexpected purity. But at this point, I was so preoccupied with my excavating that I had somewhat forgotten the world. There was a moment of panic before the immensity of the hole I had dug, immensity proportional to the distance that separated me from my contemporaries, even those I considered close to me. The excavation was not difficult for I carried it out inside myself. The real challenge was getting this source to flow freely into the world... easy to say, but to bring the absolute into the relative remains a task that few have the strength to do.

151

My most subtle ideas emanate from a light source that resides in me. I am not a channel; I don't need another being's intervention to create. It is my Being that speaks. Living in consciousness allows me to stay centered. I am not a radio station that captures and retransmits ambient waves. No! I am a creator. What I write here flows from my thoughts. I have nothing against channels; I spend time with several, but I often want to suggest they learn to think for themselves instead of letting other beings speak through them. It seems to me their statements would be better integrated. A sage is responsible for the message he shares with the world. If, on his return, the channel doesn't remember what he talked about, I don't see this as evidence of wisdom. Anything that comes from an external source only serves to make us lose our centeredness. I have thought every word I write in this book. I recognize that the source of the knowledge that I communicate comes from me and by that very fact I have already integrated it. It is rare, however, that I dissuade my friends who channel from indulging in what they enjoy doing because in general they are not really concerned about the truth as I conceive it. I bless them and do not intervene because for me it doesn't matter much, anyway.

Let them have fun in their little sandbox while those who have developed a capacity to think for themselves strive to manifest the absolute in their being unconditionally.

152

To be willfully conscious is to allow oneself to be carried by one's Being, not in the way a leaf drifts on the current, but like a captain who knows his boat and knows how to harness the power of the elements to take him to where he wants to go. This requires a great mastery of one's own self. I am not speaking here of letting myself go but of letting myself be. I flow in the direction of the current, but when it is necessary, I can row against the prevailing current because the majority is rarely carried in the direction of the truth. So I widen my scope and study the world around me attentively to ascertain the meaning of events.

153

The concept of the unconscious is fashionable today. The dominant majority seems to have come to believe that there lies in us an unconscious that serves as a sewer. It is a difficult concept to accept for someone living in consciousness. How can a part of me be unconscious if I apply myself to making my consciousness totally encompassing? How can a concept as absolute as consciousness be relativized to the point that it hides parts to itself from itself? If a part of me is unconscious I prefer to make it conscious, as I do karma. My beliefs define me and if I spend my time imagining an unconscious in me, I will certainly develop one. So do not come and talk to me about the collective unconscious, because I may sound off on you. On the whole, I prefer speaking of the subconscious and the supra-conscious, concepts that seem to me to more accurately define that part of me that has nothing to do with the physical world of everyday life.

154

Philosophy, with its constant search for truth and validity, helps me to live in a willfully conscious way. When I philosophize, I constantly define what at first glance seems indefinable. By putting words to impressions and feelings, I can better comprehend the world around me. I cultivate my intelligence as much as possible because it seems to me to be the measure of the soundness of my actions.

155

The truth finder is ostracized by truth seekers because he clamors loudly to have found what they seek. And yet the truth is there, right before our eyes, so obvious, but to feel it vibrate we must sometimes forget everything we have been taught. The one who lives in the truth is constantly in danger because lies are the rule on this planet.

156

I return again and again to this cul-de-sac that is not mine, but that of the degenerate civilization in which I live. Sometimes it seems to me that there is no other way to overcome the pain of this reality than by committing suicide. I understand those who kill themselves, for in truth this civilization is like a sinking ship. There is nothing to be done to save it. At least death offers one the power to move on to something else. And yet, I pity those who live only at the first level of thought and commit suicide physically, because they quickly understand that their torment only continues afterward. That's why I committed living suicide. A conscious suicide at least allows one to escape from the putrid vibration that makes this planet so stifling. By living in a willfully conscious way I am able to joyfully overcome the abject absurdity of this corrupt world.

157

The one who commits living suicide embraces his perfection, even at the very heart of an imperfect world. He throws away his crutches and learns to live without them. He develops intelligent ways to use his handicap and integrate it at a higher level. I use the word "handicap" in the sense that saints, geniuses and sages are rarely understood and usually considered mad. Their state of Being is of the future, not the present. They are too advanced and therefore they are the handicapped. They are the minority and unintelligible to this dominant majority that levels everything down.

I get angry at times. When that happens I unleash a holy wrath, like a patient and understanding father who, having tried everything, gets angry and raises his voice to get his children's attention. Even in conscious life, there are times when anger is the only way to send a clear signal. The anger of which I speak resembles the fury of unleashed elements like a tornado, a hurricane or a forest fire. In the natural order, these disasters also have a beneficial effect. They make room for novelty. The forest fire offers other species the chance to develop. It is obvious that this has nothing to do with the clearcutting carried out by humans, which ravages and sterilizes the land. He who applies himself to living in a willfully conscious way understands this and when anger rises in him, he is careful not to censure it. He allows it to express itself without being decentered by it. It is rather like a tornado shaking to their core the obsolete structures that have to change. The stability of our present civilization hangs by a thread, precisely because those who could make us think are drugged with narcotics or censored to the point that their cries of rage are not heard. May all those who desire real change on this planet lend an ear, only then will they hear the cry of Being.

159

He who lives in a willfully conscious manner is formidable. He has nothing left to lose because he has already renounced all that is not essential. He remains centered on what is permanent and therein lies his strength. In a world where impermanence is glorified in every way, it's obvious he will be disruptive. This explains why beings such as Christ or Socrates were so severely condemned. But by whom were they condemned? By those, of course, whom the principle of impermanence serves the most. How is it that we still use oil or electricity when Tesla discovered a clean, renewable form of energy nearly a hundred years ago? The manipulative plutocratic system is only too happy to stave a hole in the hull of the ship that is our civilization, to sell us another. We will have to shout together a "No, thank you!" with all our might to stop it from further rotting our existence. The problem, however, is that its propaganda has been so effective that humans have come to believe that impermanence is part of their nature. That's why we have a desperate need for sages.

160

He who lives in a willfully conscious way will not actively meddle in the world. Like Gandhi, he will change himself and let the world gallop to its doom with a smile. A conscious smile is always worth more than unconscious and blind anger. The enlightened one sees the world as it is, in its perfection. He will not act unless his Being inspires it, then only will he do it, but with such detachment that one can say that everything is done in him.

Conscious life is rare in this world. By perniciously interfering in our education, our intimacy and our thoughts, the manipulative plutocratic system eliminates all possibility of awakening to consciousness. I know several people who have experienced white light or had lucid dreams, but most of them did not understand that they had to anchor these experiences in the relative in order to recover the feeling of the absolute. Some desperately sought from their environment a validation of their experience... in vain. Some looked to religion, and of course those they consulted were careful not to redirect them to the mystical branches of their religions, such as Kabbalah and Sufism. These schools teach concrete practices to secure the absolute in oneself. It is painful to hear testimonies of people who came so close to awakening but who went back to sleep almost immediately. Some told me that in their childhood they could see the invisible and because of their family's lack of support and understanding, they eventually stopped Seeing. These experiences would have made me very unhappy had I not learned to see the world through the eyes of the Living God.

171

Too many people are afraid of sects today. It is an atavism of what prompted humans to burn witches in the Middle Ages and torture geniuses throughout history. Luckily for me, I do not identify with humanity, for I would be ashamed. I prefer to consider myself a being of an energetic essence vacationing on a handicapped planet that is out of control and perpetually testing my will to stay conscious. I must constantly remain willfully conscious not to go mad. This fear of sects, which is in fact the fear of the unknown, is a result of the ignorance prevalent in this world. I am not talking here about intellectual or academic understanding. There have been illiterate sages, like Ramakrishna. Knowledge has nothing to do with understanding, for it comes from within, emanating from Being without reason. The one who Knows does not need to understand, and if he becomes a scientist it is only for the pleasure of it, because his essence is already complete. I have come to trust my intuitions, my feelings and all that I cannot explain rationally but which represents a wild certainty. I am not afraid of the unknown because nothing is unknown to me. I have a sense of perpetual complicity with reality. I always know my way. I do not need the pity of others. I know I Am, I know where I am going and, to my utmost despair, it seems to me that I am headed in a radically different direction from my contemporaries.

172

A great anger surges in me and if I do not express it here, I'm afraid the fury may carry me away. The wind lifts and tears away all in me that is not fixed in permanence. I am gentle and patient; I reach out and give seekers a chance, but at some point I have to lift myself up to find my center. They exhaust me, all these chronically decentered people who offend me with their ignorance, I who Know and yet cannot make them understand.

173

Today I went to a party to please my partner, but before long I realized that the other guests had no Being. I felt so alone among those shadows! It was the straw that broke the camel's back. I came home with a mighty headache. I tried to sleep but the only solution to appease the anger was to continue writing this book. I am not ashamed of this anger; it is justified and understandable (at least to me). Luckily, since my childhood, I have developed an effective method to prevent this violence from being destructive: art. I project this violence towards the well-oiled machine of my imagination to sublimate it into creative violence. The feverish intensity I produce allows others to warm themselves and become enlightened. Knowing this, I provoke myself to multiply the violence that would undoubtedly destroy me if I did not master it. I had an intense headache all day which culminated in this party where I did not feel respected. And after nine pages of wrathful writing, I finally feel the rage subside. This violence resides in each of us. Wisdom rests in the ability to sublimate it before it levels us or has us say or do destructive things. Yes, I am a raving madman, but at least I am aware of it!

174

To rely on the general law to guide you is the equivalent of shooting yourself in the foot. The general law is stupid. It dumbs everything down. It is easy to understand why the one who adheres to the law of exception loses all reference in a world where the common denominator is the collective consent to applaud the ordinary, the tasteless and the insipid. It is like a drain that sucks you inexorably into the sewer called civilization. Luckily, I have the energy of despair to lift me out of this cesspool. I constantly encounter free-falling bodies that cling to me on their way down. They slow and weigh me down. That's why I decided to discontinue the evolutionary journey. I sit in the center of myself, conscious of having arrived, conscious that even if I were to stumble into the filth, I would remain serene and centered on the infinite source of light that grows in me every day.

175

Though I may be terribly irritated at the moment, I remain happy and serene. What a paradox, you say! And yet, if I examine the feeling that inhabits me now, it is definitely one of subtle harmony. Why? Because I create. The creator that I am feeds on this contrast to transform it into something rich that will serve to empower my community. In that resides precisely the difference between art and therapy. I am not sick, I am a master.

176

I can transform the foulest garbage into the most stunning jewelry without leaving a trace of its origin. Look at a butterfly with a magnifying glass and there is no trace of the caterpillar it once was. Art therapy simply spreads the shit without sublimating it; in the end, it remains shit, even if it is now a sculpture. Real art is alchemical. There is transformation—sublimation. The artist takes the shit and turns it into gold. He erases all traces of the old. The miraculous catalyst of the process is consciousness.

177

Consciousness is what distinguishes human beings from other species. Through its permanence, consciousness infuses into the human a quality which is normally far beyond him. He becomes familiar with the presence of the absolute within, which leads him to create a permanent center of gravity. Thus, the person gives himself a Being and, patiently, makes it grow until it fills him. If this individual is intelligent in addition to being wise, he will know how to juxtapose his person to his Being instead of killing it. He who lives in a willfully conscious way loses almost all traces of humanity, for divinity fills him to the brim. And if at times it yields ground to the self, it is always strategic—to make him feel even more intensely his Being. To give oneself a Being is impossible in this world. That is why the man who succeeds necessarily follows the law of exception... because the exception confirms the rule.

178

I have written furiously for three hours and my headache is finally gone. I did not know what to do with myself so I put myself to work. The faster I write, the clearer my thoughts. At this speed, I leap over the obstacles and trappings of morality. I write so fast that my mind does not have time to follow. Inspiration brings me where I want to go and the words come out naturally, precise and polished. I am pleased to have sketched so many pages in my comic book series, Abstractions. The absence of words allows me to touch in me an infinite potential of creation that frees itself from the weight of rationality. And now that I apply my inspiration to something as rational as words, I can sublimate them. My words bear something much more subtle and profound: my thoughts. The world of ideas is eternal, beyond time or space. That's why I feel so good and familiar within it. My thoughts precede my self. I profoundly enjoy this absolute knowledge which springs from me without concession. I possess a fierce intensity. I am wild in the sense that I am not civilized; I am not programmed or controlled. It is my deepest conviction that I am ungovernable.

179

To live in a willfully conscious way is not trivial. I would even say it borders on the miraculous, and yet it is possible for the person who thinks about it incessantly to change the function of his self, somewhat like turning a glove inside out. Inside becomes outside and we realize that we are separated from nothing, that every detail is in its place in the Great Whole... even the flaws that irritate us. He who lives in this way no longer looks at reality in the same way. Though he fixes his gaze on the same reality as normal people, his perception is more subtle, more piercing. The invisible has burst through into the ordinary and the enlightened one lives constantly at the junction of the visible and the invisible. In some cultures the divine is part of everyday life, but in the West, wary be he who governs himself under the law of exception because he will not be well received! He will be misunderstood by his friends and his family. But in the state that he is in, he no longer needs the approval of others. He is a free electron.

180

My senses are inflamed. I perceive the world with such clarity! There are so many things I could do with these perceptions, but my Being constantly reminds me to curb my enthusiasm. I don't want to end up in prison or crucified. I don't want to expose my flank to assaults unnecessarily. So I work on myself. I am my most interesting project, a real laboratory where nothing is off-limits. My consciousness fills the space. It even gets uncomfortable at times. I feel cramped among these narrow and tone-deaf human beings. I realize that never during my lifetime will I be able to make myself understood by this comatose majority. It bothers me less and less. I am so vast now!

181

Nothing and no one can stop the one who lives in a willfully conscious way because he is no longer of this world. He no longer obeys laws of consensus for he has established himself in the absolute. Obstacles are nothing to him because, like water, he can infiltrate cracks and find his way despite adversity. He is in contact with the invisible every second. When the tiger passes, he is elsewhere. He is also like the wind, intangible, immaterial. He moves ahead on the path effortlessly because he does not progress, he does not evolve. He is content to be, and if his Being tells him to turn left, he does so without hesitation. If a wall blocks his path, he sits without emotion and waits for an opportunity to present itself for him to pass through. Opportunities are always there for him, and even if they do not come, he is not disturbed because he has arrived. This being has nothing more to do because everything happens inside him.

182

To live in a willfully conscious way you have to know how to listen to yourself. The voice of intuition is entrenched in me. I know what I have to do. I know where I'm going. I don't hesitate. My path has been laid out for a long time and I just follow it like a train on tracks. I just need to be careful in the curves, to slow down at the right time. My advantage is that I'm in no hurry. It is the hasty people who derail. In wanting to save time, in going too fast, they end up having accidents that ultimately cause them to waste a lot of time and often even force them to stop. Since I am committed to wrap each of my actions in consciousness, I almost always succeed in avoiding disaster. And if someone has laid a tree trunk on the tracks, I bless him. I perform a miracle and at the last minute a friend of my essence removes the trunk for me and I continue on my crazy adventure. Rational logic doesn't function in the absolute. The only thing that counts is what a person has given himself to be. That being established, everything conspires to make it happen. Consciousness, being beyond time and space, has privileged access to everything that constitutes the film of the reality in which the self is the actor. For me there is no plan B, there is only my Being's plan, and I would not stray from it for anything in the world.

183

To be conscious is above all to understand that the physical world is only the tip of a giant iceberg, the bulk of which is invisible to the uneducated eye. In the center of our brain is situated a third eye that has all the characteristics of our two physical eyes... except that of being turned towards the outside world. The pineal gland is an eye turned in on itself that allows us to see the inner world. We see dreams with it. It is also responsible for perceiving the invisible through telepathy, intuition, mediumship or clairvoyance. To live in consciousness we must activate all our senses, even the most subtle ones, because only then can consciousness be truly in contact with reality. He who lives in consciousness no longer feels separate from anything which grants him privileged access to knowledge. Without necessarily being aware that someone has laid a trap for him, he won't fall into it simply by being unavailable. His want-to-be killer will himself be killed on route to the crime. The finite person is cut off from the world and has no access to this privileged knowledge. This is why life on earth is a disaster of solitude and suffering. To live consciously is to open all the senses and perceive the world as it is, without trying to change it. Like water that takes the shape of its recipient, the enlightened one takes the shape of the world in which he lives, drawing the maximum from this stifling prison which he recognizes as being a representation at the core of consciousness.

184

If you want to live in a willfully conscious way, don't look for points of reference around you because you won't find them. Our civilization is poorer than ever at this level. Yoga centers that teach you to evolve, to purify yourself, are easy to come by. Then one day you will understand that all this does not lead to consciousness but only to an interminable spiritual journey. Out of despair, you may decide to capitulate and enter into yourself to understand that you have already arrived, that there is nothing to do because consciousness is beyond life, beyond all journeying. A being does not evolve towards consciousness; he is already there as soon as he is constituted in the world. Too naive to think for himself, he accepts without question everything that he is taught and arrives at a critical juncture where he forgets his true nature. So, my friends, if you really want to live in consciousness, stop evolving and settle here and now in consciousness, without accepting steps and without trying to deserve it, because consciousness is the most natural thing there is. Unfortunately, many of us must reach a critical point of despair to finally capitulate. If only our parents lived in consciousness when we are born! They could at least help us stay in touch with it from a very young age, at a stage of our development where we still feel one with everything.

185

If, instead of sending us to kindergarten and primary school, we were placed in a context that would allow us to stay in touch with consciousness, it would be much easier for us, as adults, to live in a willfully conscious manner. It would be second nature to perceive the invisible world. Continuity and permanence would be faithful companions. We could teach it to young ones and help reality on Earth be more harmonious. We would always be in the right place at the right time. The world I am describing is not yet possible. There is too much resistance and the few who already live this way cannot keep everyone awake. This is why enlightened ones generally content themselves to let the few students who want to receive their teachings come to them. Consciousness is not of this world. Matter is so opaque. And for the majority it is impossible to live in consciousness because everything in their life is strategically placed to distract them from it. Indeed, it is time for parents to take responsibility, to refuse to subject their children to the education system, to refuse to work forty hours or more per week and to devote themselves to educating their children to remain conscious. Those who are not willing to do so should not have children. It is a blatant lack of maturity to let children be desensitized by the manipulative plutocratic system. I prefer not to have children than see them lose consciousness in a school system designed to turn them into nine-to-five, five-day a-week robots, and to reproduce the same pattern when they enter the workplace. None of this has anything to do with consciousness.

186

In order to learn to live in a willfully conscious way, we can choose to constantly reflect on permanence. Little by little, we can arrange it so that this principle becomes central to all that we undertake; our projects, friendships, work and intimate relationships. I constantly ask myself this question: will this or that lead me to establish permanence in my life? I want permanence in everything because it is the only way I can create a permanent center of gravity. If I don't pay attention to permanence in my human life, how can I claim immortality? One does not hope for immortality, one decides it! And we act accordingly by establishing concrete practice in our daily life. Anything goes to remind me that nothing is more important than permanence. I feel that I can live forever, not as a human being but as a being of an energetic essence. I am so little of this world that at times it confuses me. I look around and see only impermanence. Everything collapses and like a madman I cling to the concept of permanence so as not to be carried away in this current that extols the ephemeral.

187

The civilization in which I live is ephemeral. It is not meant to last. And I who wants to live in permanence, I am left to my own devices. They call me a madman, a dreamer, a fool because I want to live with several women and create an elected family that can offer me a stability conducive to feeling the infinite grow inside me. People today prefer successive loves. It does not lead anywhere, we must always start over. It is contrary to what I believe. I do not want romantic relationships to follow one another in my life. I want them to juxtapose and multiply. I want to live simultaneously and permanently with friends of a shared essence. But I am constantly confronted with the resistance of civilized people. The idea that someone has the wisdom to be loved by several partners at the same time is intolerable to them because they are incapable of it. Should I live like a disabled person because my contemporaries are that, and because they are the majority, it has become the norm? In this sense I am not normal. I understood that a long time ago and I assume responsibility for my difference. I can live this way now, but it is a constant challenge because I am not understood and my companions are constantly tested by the morals of their friends and family. My values are not of this world. Now that I have understood that, I no longer seek to mold myself to the world; on the contrary, I force it to adjust to me.

188

I intentionally use the word "willfully" because living in consciousness draws on the will. Indeed, it is through my own will that I set in motion the auto-movement of Being, which in turn constantly renews the source of energy which is my will. My desire to live in a willfully conscious way arises from my self's obsessive need to revert to its true nature, which is energetic. I stay away from emotions that cloud my perception. Knowing myself as a being of an energetic essence places all temporal considerations in their place, that is, on the tip of the iceberg. So I do not suppress emotions, I relativize them, because I know that above them are feelings, which guide me toward my center. They bring me back to the truth. I am always attentive to my feelings because they have their origin in the most subtle part of what I Am. If consciousness is a boat, then feelings are the rudder. If in doubt, I can rely on them to right my course. The will then is the captain who stays the course by maneuvering the rudder.

189

The will is necessary to realize an undertaking as crazy as enlightenment. I want to anchor this in my life in a tangible way so as never to forget it. That's why my new TV show project is called The Will of Happiness. Happiness is an act of will. It takes a Herculean effort to establish oneself vertically to this world while everyone else is content to dwell in the horizontal. Once we reach the peak of ourselves, we must constantly renew our will. This is the most difficult part. To awaken is an easy task, but to remain so, at the heart of a civilization of sleepers, is a real challenge. I have met people who experienced the white light but, failing to integrate it in their life, fell back into ignorance—it's less painful than to watch one's life collapse like a house of cards. My will is stronger than all else; it is nourished by a thunderous energy which I use to propel myself into consciousness... and remain there in spite of all adversity.

190

A sublime happiness emanates from every pore of my skin. It is a wild certainty which lifts me towards the "heights of despair," as Cioran so eloquently put it. But for me, it is a luminous and splendid despair that frees me from all expectations. I do not expect anything from this world, but by remaining open, I welcome the surprises that come to me and that warm my heart. This is what keeps me alive, because life in the mind is cold and disembodied. It would be easy for me to lose interest in the world if not for the incentives I receive every day to stay. He who has known ecstasy can easily detach himself from the world of humans, which is so painful and imperfect. He who lives in a willfully conscious way is free to leave because he has understood the essence of reality; he is able to put it in context. He knows he will outlive his person, which he no longer identifies with anyway.

191

The self is like a microscope; it is an organ of multisensory perception. Without the finite self, how can I feel the infinite palpitate in me? My self is a platform from which I can dive into infinity and return to savor wondrous gifts. For too many people, this platform is shaky and unstable. They cannot invest themselves with the absolute, for they know deep down that the return would be very difficult or impossible. That is why I consider my self sacred. It is the receptacle of the divine and therefore divine.

192

Conscious life is a paradox. Life is finite, ephemeral and relative, whereas consciousness is beyond time and space. It is absolute, infinite. To live in a willfully conscious way one must integrate the paradox and be able to see that at a higher level, opposites coexist. I can thus be the universe while the universe is in me. These are not opposed because I can perceive reality without the yoke of the mind, which obliges me to reduce everything to duality—that the one and the other are distinct. I am the eye that sees itself. It is impossible to conceive it rationally. Which came first, the chicken or the egg? It's enough to bedevil the mind, unless you have been initiated into the paradox. Thus the answer follows: the chicken and the egg appear at the same time in my consciousness, without cause, without logic, for the sole pleasure of being perceived by me.

Because I suffuse my acts with consciousness, I don't concern myself with the notion of "error." I don't make mistakes because I let my Being take care of everything. I have imprinted in golden letters on my mind the concept of strategic movement. My Being leads me to where I need to be and so far I have always been in the right place at the right time. This has allowed me to skip steps because my mind is not dominated by linear reality. No matter how I attain the pinnacle of myself, the important thing for me is to be there. Those who want to climb with sweat and tears are free to do so. I will not intervene, but if they ask my opinion, then I answer that there are no steps to arrive at consciousness because it is there at every moment, ready to be grasped. Humans waste their time evolving. They do not feel worthy. And initiates who claim that it is better to be evolved than to evolve are rarely taken seriously and too often persecuted. Humans have come to believe that we must be worthy of consciousness, when in fact it is the primordial principle from which springs life. They believe they make mistakes that must be forgiven by God before being worthy of inner peace or access to heaven. I give myself this inner peace here and now. Why wait, when even the concept of waiting has no meaning, time being an illusion? Consciousness returns to the fore when my will sets my Being in motion, inevitably returning me to the absolute. How can I be ecstatic if part of me holds me back in the dark? I discard all notions of karma and I throw myself into the absolute without ulterior motive.

194

Doubt and hesitation don't apply to consciousness. Resistance comes from the grossest levels. The laws of physics wear me down to remind me of my end as a physical object. I am only the pilot of this object. If I so desire, I will exchange it for another when it wears out. I have an infinite number of simultaneous lives that I intend to use to ensure my permanence. Doubt slows us down; it distracts us from the essential. The mind does not recognize the truth when it sees it. That is why I trust my feelings. I still consult my mind because sometimes its interpretation is relevant, but ultimately I rely on my intuition. In this respect, I don't apologize when I am reproached for something. I stand firm despite the evidence, confident that someday what appeared to be a mistake will prove to be a strategic movement of my Being.

195

Living in a willfully conscious way inevitably leads to Seeing the world through the eyes of the Living God. I perceive a thin immaterial film of subtle light. I feel it more than I see it. My physical eyes are too coarse. I cannot rely on them because this light that I perceive is so fine, so soft and enticing that I cannot determine its origin. If I light the lamp in front of me, I understand that the light emanates from the incandescent bulb. But this subtle light has no cause. It fills my apartment. It vibrates like a wild certainty. It is my whole Being that perceives it. I feel so light, so pure. And the more I focus on it, the more clearly I understand that this light emanates from me. I emit this light and yet it seems at the same time to exist by itself. I feel so light, my head is spinning. I used neither drugs, nor alcohol and yet I'm drunk. It seems evident to me at this moment that I am evolved, that it is enough for me to let myself be so that more waves of light surge in me and overwhelm me with their voluptuousness. Joy is such a sweet feeling. I feel the infinite in me. I vibrate with it and my mind understands it. I grasp the unfathomable because I permit myself all the whims, even the one to invest myself with the absolute, to be one with it. My perceptions are so clear; I enjoy in silence the beauty that my eyes of flesh cannot even see. I See all the subtleties of infinite time converging on my heart that suddenly wants to burst.

196

The infinite source of consciousness I discovered in me a few years ago overflows from the finite limits of my self. It is perceptible to those who have altered the function of their eyes. This validates in a way my deepest conviction: I am a source of infinite light. And taking into account where I am, I have only to shine like a sun. Nothing else really matters; as long as I am shining I am what I've set out to be. All these people who await the permission of others to shine have understood nothing. Does the sun ask permission to radiate?

When I radiate like a sun, I attract beings who place themselves in orbit around me. I appreciate them without trying to transform them into suns, too. A system is composed of numerous elements, which, taken together, form a whole. I content myself to radiate and observe life appear on some of these planets. Even dead planets serve a purpose in the balance of the Great All. I have the wisdom to let the exceptional ones into my orbit. I let them grow accustomed to my radiance and benefit from it. I give without asking anything in return because for the majority of people, the first step to being able to give is learning to receive. At one point in my life I believed I had to be poor to be a true artist and that led me to a dead end. I had the good fortune to meet a sun that was content to give me gifts without asking anything in exchange. And slowly, I grew accustomed to abundance. This gave me strength to finally become a sun myself. After years of taking, I finally reached a state in which I felt so complete, so full, that the abundance of the infinite began to overflow. It is now my turn to radiate bountifully. Inevitably, individuals have begun to gravitate to me. Some are visible and some are not. The Being I have given myself is still unintelligible to them, but they come to feel it, and without realizing it, they gravitate to me. All this amuses me because I went through it, too. I therefore rejoice at the influence I have over them. I lend them some of my Being to accustom them to abundance and one day perhaps they will be the ones to radiate and create their own system. But it matters little to me. I just radiate and bless them.

198

In this book, I am constantly repeating these words of power: live in a willfully conscious way. I hammer them home in me so that they remain imprinted there forever. I think this thought every moment. I dream of it and make it a subject of discussion with those who cross my path. I feel I must constantly repeat them until they become totally integrated with what I Am, like those who repeat a dance move ad infinitum so that when the time comes, they can forget it and be carried away by inspiration. Despite the vigorous intensity of my will, the civilization in which I live has very effective methods to incite us to live without consciousness. It is so easy to abdicate and to let oneself be governed by the system until death. Thousands of years have perfected the desensitization that is at its apex today. And yet, many people believe they are masters of their lives. They don't feel the bars of the prison inside which they run around in circles, unable to leave. I existed in my wild state long enough to free myself. I am not impressed by scholars who can recite an entire dictionary from memory. If they don't have the intelligence to create themselves, in the end, I don't think I really have anything to learn from them. I have met super-intellectuals. They are brilliant, but too often handicapped in areas not their specialty. I can respect the intelligence of someone who knows how to be loved, who has loving partners or who knows how to promote harmony and joy in his life. So when I remind myself to live in a willfully conscious way, I especially want to remember to suffuse all aspects of what I Am with consciousness. In this way I won't be a handicapped specialist.

199

If I were to specialize too much, I would become vulnerable, so I constantly try to find new ways to make money, express myself and attract abundance. I constantly renew my desire to share my life with several women. In this way I am more stable in all aspects of my life. If a woman or a client leaves me, there is always another to fill the void and prevent me from acting like a victim. Even though my main source of income is website design and infographics, I constantly imagine ways to attract abundance that do not involve the Internet, electricity or even money. If a disaster were to cut off all communication, I could sing, sell my books, give lectures, and so on. It is precisely because I suffuse all my actions with consciousness that I can step back from the world and not fall into the plutocrats' trap, which incites us to specialize to better manipulate us. I am difficult to manipulate, whether in business, love or friendship, because I stand at the center of myself. I am not dependent on anyone in particular. I constantly give myself new options. If I want to live eternally, I must know how to renew myself. Things change so fast. You have to be able to follow the current and skillfully surf the chaos of the modern world, otherwise you may get left behind.

To not specialize does not mean not doing what
I am best at. On the contrary, I take full advantage of it. But, by reflex, I imagine crisis sce-
narios because it helps me generate new ideas
and remain creative. Although my Being is
eternal, down here impermanence reigns. And
so, if I want to live a human life, I have to play
the game. It took me nearly thirty-two years to
understand this. The cul-de-sac in which I found
myself gave me a taste of limitation. I realized
that I never wanted to end up dependent on the
state and my friends again. I know that during
my human life I will have to remain vigilant
and never let anyone imprison me and wea-
ken me by wanting to complete me. Let it be
clear, I am complete and I will remain so. Those
who wish to live with me will have to content
themselves with being extras. I put to work the
conscious energy that inhabits me and let my
Being provide me with the abundance of the
infinite. I will not want for anything because I
apply myself to being rich with the infinite by
thinking like a millionaire. My wealth is not
specialized; it is what gives me the feeling of
being free. Of course, I make money but I also
barter, invest in the printing of my books and
paint canvases that I will sell one day. I have
infinite resources. I am centered at the level of
the absolute and totally off-center at the relative level. Someone who wants to hurt me by
no longer doing business with me will be surprised if I tell him that at the exact moment
he let his intentions be known, another client
was boasting of my services elsewhere. It is by

remaining conscious that I can live from the abundance of the infinite. It incites me to want to be just, and the one who is just cannot be robbed of anything. That which belongs to him will be returned to him by the law of compensation. Unfortunately, specialists have no understanding of this nonlinear law.

201

Despite my repeated attempts to teach others the art of giving themselves options, in practice virtually no one has the courage to take action. They prefer to spend forty hours a week doing the same thing. And of course their love life resembles their professional life. It goes without saying that it is difficult to take them seriously when they speak to me of consciousness. They go to their yoga classes to stretch a little and relax their consciousness, but after class they return to their usual poverty. I gave up trying. Now I take good care of myself. I diversify endlessly and leave my friends the freedom to choose the life they want. But they had better not complain to me the day they lose their job or divorce. I realize that on this planet, intelligence is not the norm. All these civilized people think themselves so intelligent with their technological gadgets-cum-prostheses, until they are left in a lurch when they lose them. Intelligence is rather the ability of a person to prioritize himself in both the short, and the long-term.

When you live in a willfully conscious way, it inevitably leads you to mind your own business. Humans are so bereft of harmony; to be at peace it is better to remain the impassive observer of the world. It doesn't mean you make yourself invisible or stop speaking your mind. Rather, you let yourself be, and above all, you apply this rule to others. So I distance myself from those who desperately seek out problems. If they ask me for advice, I share my point of view but I am careful not to get actively involved in solving their conflicts. It is sometimes difficult. I get caught in a situation and before I can even turn away, I am involved. And then comes the moment when the clutter of troubles brings up in me a powerful impulse of rejection. So, as a whole, I disinvest from everything that is not essential. I do not forget my dreams. Those that disrupt me in real life tend to do so also in my dreams. I then make it clear to those who lack harmony that I do not accept being entrapped against my will in situations that do not concern me. I am no longer concerned with the fate of mankind as a whole. I see it as a representation of which I must remain lucid and conscious so as not to invent stories that have nothing to do with my entelechy.

203

Consciousness is a realm of manifestation and living consciously allows me to relativize the world while remaining totally integrated in it. I look at the landscape around me; through a grace my mind cannot grasp, I not only perceive it, but appreciate it as well. I could run at full speed with my eyes riveted to the ground, already visualizing my destination, but in so doing I would miss out on the pleasure of observing the passing landscape. I place myself at the center of the world and watch it move around me. In reality I am immobile. I capitulated and I sat down at the center of myself. It is easy now for me to understand that the world is a representation in infinite flux in front of my consciousness. I take the time to observe it, to appreciate it. I no longer move; I let the world move in me... it is much less of a struggle. Ease is proof of harmony.

204

To live in a willfully conscious way means to stop "evolving" and be content with inner journeys. Every part of me is near the absolute. I do not think I need to evolve. It is an absurd idea that prevents too many people from enjoying the here and now. I can do this because I have given myself a Being and foster its growth in me. I let it take its place and thus annihilate any desire to "progress" to be satisfied and happy. Of course, at the first level of thought, I may be dissatisfied by such and such a situation, but it is so superficial a feeling that it never curtails the ultimate satisfaction of having found in me an inexhaustible source of light.

205

This source of immanent light is what convinces me, more than anything, that it is worth giving myself a Being and cherishing my self despite the imperfections of the Earthly plane. I am the reason for my presence here and now. I enjoy myself beyond measure. I am the instrument of the sweetest pleasures. Through my piercing intellect I understand this so powerfully that I enter into ecstasy. More than ever, I feel the light emanate from me and create a sort of mist of clarity. This may seem paradoxical, and yet this phenomenon seems to change the world around me at the molecular level. Harmony down to the most subtle levels brings me a sublime peace which, as I crystallize it through my art, creates an oasis beyond compare. Little by little this oasis is populated by friends of my essence... my elected family.

206

I imbue the world with what I Am. The joy I feel spreads around me through capillarity. And thanks to my art, it can travel to the four corners of the world. What I Am vastly surpasses my person. Because I am fixed in permanence, the most primitive anxieties are eliminated. This is unintelligible to my contemporaries. They live day-to-day, which is normal given that they believe they are descendants of apes. They are nothing but civilized animals. As for me, I'm a thinking light. I shine in all directions without seeking a goal for my actions. I no longer want to feel separate from anything. The other is me.

There is no separation in the infinite that I Am. And yet I also intensely feel my individuality. It is the integration of this paradox at higher and higher planes that causes light to emanate irresistibly from me. This has a stabilizing effect. By making myself so vast, the permanent center of gravity that I constantly nourish with my intention fluctuates less and less.

207

I am exultant. These words I write feverishly are like ballast I jettison for my balloon to rise. I want to be at the pinnacle of myself to See the world through the eyes of the Living God. I want to take leave of the relative for a short time to dissolve into the absolute I Am. I release my companions and partners so that they too can accept that I do not need them because they are only an extension of my self, a supplement in the infinite that I Am. This exultation is the sign that my life is harmonious and that I can safely be drunk with my Being, without risk of injury. I know I am consciousness. I know I am light and that is what breaks the moorings and propels me to the peaks of my spirit. Perched on this summit, I enjoy in silence, writing for posterity, far from humans and their imperfections. I am going through a period of such intensity that nothing can resist this forward thrust. I find it difficult to tolerate those who hold me back through their ignorance or bad faith. I am annoyed by these vampires who believe they can get in my way without suffering consequences. I went so far in my psychedelic experiences! I have not forgotten the way or the feeling of leaving the physical world. Joy seems to me to be the highest feeling, and it is because I am consciously aware that I can feel it so clearly.

208

I can scarcely put into words the indescribable feeling of voluptuousness that uplifts me. Yet I have never felt so irritated by the primitive behavior of my contemporaries. It probably serves as a dense limit that propels me towards the most subtle planes of my self, the planes without form where my spirit spreads over the world like a cloud. Even though I still feel the emotions, I manage to integrate them on a higher plane. Thus, anger, irritation and dissatisfaction do not taint this sense of harmony that fills me. I watch these emotions pass through me but they do not seem mine. They are too foreign for me to consider them mine. They pass, that's all, and I observe them with vigilance because I know that here emotions wear on me and make me sick. I accept that and focus on my feelings. And here and now, it is a feeling of lightness and joy that dominates my thoughts. I feel alone because I understand that everything around me is an extension of me, even those who irritate me with their presence. I have reached a state that cannot be improved. I have nothing else to do and it is sufficient for me to simply be for eternity.

209

I let the world come to me. I'm so well at home, in my center. I ask friends of my essence, and especially woman friends, not to be angry with me if I prefer the sweetness of my apartment to bars and noisy parties. I'm so sensitive right now; I'm completely focused on consciousness. I watch it fill my apartment with a luminous mist that confirms my feeling of joy. Of course, I don't expect to be totally understood by those who love me. I write my books in hopes they will read them to better understand that they cannot consider me a normal person, because normality rhymes with mediocrity and banality. Everything is different on subtle levels. I would be delighted to be considered normal if being normal meant being conscious. I continue to create with all my strength, except I expend practically no energy promoting my books. I constantly seek ease. If I cannot sell my books, then I give them away. And little by little, I spread out into the world; my ideas and my thoughts have their own life and they are the ones that make their way out into the world, not me. I remain motionless, happy and content; I let this light source that grows in me spill out. Every conscious gesture adds to those I have already made. It's not that hard, but to get there, you have to give yourself time to Be. The quality moments that I offer myself, to be with myself and with those I value, are diamonds from which I fashion a necklace. I have destroyed in me all desire for social success, so if I receive any in this lifetime, I will simply appreciate it instead of keeping my nose to the grindstone to acquire more. I no longer have ambition. It works in my favor because, when I create, I can be totally present to myself. I write to make myself happy, to do me good, and so my friends can understand me better. I want them to accept that they are dealing with a man who has devoted himself completely to establishing himself in permanence.

210

A soft light grows in me. It is the flower of my consciousness. I am moved by so much beauty. It is I who secrete it with remarkable steadiness. Since I was ten years old, I have never lacked inspiration. I have always known how to renew myself. Then, at twenty-eight, it took on cosmic proportions. Every day I feel vaster, more eternal. I strive by every possible means to integrate consciousness into every one of my actions, and because I do it so well I have begun to teach it to those I love who are open to me. Unfortunately, most of those who love me are not open. They have formulated an idea of who I am, which prevents them from understanding that I Am. I don't hold it against them. I remain attentive to them when they approach so that they don't break something without realizing it. The more my intelligence grows, the less I expect my contemporaries to understand me. It seems such an impossible task that I capitulate. I have come to believe that the most important thing is for me to understand what I Am and express it as clearly as possible in my work. Some privileged people will understand that it is time to listen to the sages; they are the only ones who don't have a short-term agenda because they are less concerned about outcomes than about how they exist.

211

I have long felt like a lie detector. And with my ever heightening sensitivity, it feels like I come face-to-face with lies at every turn. I am a truth-loving person and the omnipresent lies of the world torment me. When I hear a politician or an advertisement, I become tense, angry and irritated. I watch emotions grow inside me without being able to do anything about it. Most humans are liars and hurtful hypocrites. Lying is systemic and the citizens are fooled by it. When I hear people bleating, for example, that the Arabs are all terrorists, I have to restrain myself not to vomit. I understand then how effective the propaganda of the manipulative plutocratic system is and how it shapes the world. Because I live in a willfully conscious way, I have a backstage pass to the world; I see behind the scenes; I understand the tricks of magicians because I see them from an angle that is not accessible to those who are not conscious of the truth. Frankly, I don't even want to try convincing them that they are getting the wool pulled over their eyes. What good is it to try to convince a blind man that he is standing before the most sublime artwork? The truth has never been accessible to the majority. It is a fact and I don't feel the imperative to rub their face in it. Yet my art contains truths which might well convince some. So much the better if that happens, but that's not what drives me to create fiercely since my childhood. I am simply moved by the desire for beauty which is in itself its own reward.

He who develops the ability to detect lies will always be one step ahead. If he stays attentive, he will be elsewhere when the tiger passes. When separation from the outside world dissolves, consciousness gives access to knowledge. I only know what I need to know. Wild certainty arises in me and I have no choice but to pay attention. Animals are more likely to be attentive to this phenomenon. They know and do not waste time with guesswork. They act. And the awakened man is like an animal, except that he can reflect on this knowledge, which compels him to pay attention. I no longer try to understand why I sometimes feel irritated with someone or a situation. I learned that when it happens, it is a sign of a lack of harmony underlying the person or situation. To prevent the absence of harmony from staining me, I forcefully send a clear message that lying is odious and that it better not be imposed on me. I know that I am not the only one like this on the planet. Our number grows every day. Soon we will be united so that together we will form the most powerful lie detector in history.

213

I consciously observe emotions rise in me and then dissipate. I understand there's nothing I can do, so I don't try to control them. I let them grow and then dissolve, for lack of a reason to persist. There is a lot of anger in me right now. One medium told me that in one of my reincarnations (which I prefer to call simultaneous lives), I was unjustly imprisoned and it cost me my life. She then felt terrible anger at this injustice and bewilderment before such an absurd destiny. I know that I am boundless and that my present self communicates from within with other simultaneous lives. That is why I don't identify with all the emotions that arise in me. Sometimes they seem so unrelated to my present life that they astonish me. Living in a willfully conscious way gives me a great advantage. I am not ashamed of these passing emotions; I do not try to hold them back. They come and go like ocean waves, but what I Am is established in the peaceful depths of my Being.

214

Once humans understand that emotions have nothing to do with consciousness, they will stop suffering and eventually stop dying. Disease stems from unintegrated emotions, as do wars and conflicts. We must learn to be the witness of ourselves, to no longer identify ourselves with this machine. When I drive a car or ride a bicycle, I know that I am only the driver. It is the same with my person that is only the vehicle for the expression of consciousness. To understand this is to accept immortality as possible, is to allow oneself to see the world through the eyes of the Living God.

215

The most difficult emotion is undoubtedly love—love that others have for us. This emotion, sticky like syrup, is difficult to avoid. As soon as I begin a loving relationship, the beloved suddenly wants to occupy my entire space, as if I had to disown all others I love and who were there long before her. I found an effective way to cool the possessive ardor of women who want to become my companion: the first two years, I consider them friends... which is already a lot. A friend is more open and understanding; she understands that she has no right to possess me. That seems to me the smartest way to build lasting relationships. The majority go too fast today. They have no discernment. They get married quickly and divorce after a few years. How pathetic they are! Real children! This two-year probation period seems to me necessary to establish a true energetic relationship without the unbearable harmonics of jealousy and the desire to cut the other off from everything. When the women of my life grow impatient with this title of friend, which they say is not strong enough, I take the opportunity to remind them that it's better for them to get to know me before declaring promises of eternal love. I put them to the test by introducing them to the other women I want to add to my love life. I give them my books so that they can study my ideas and make sure they really want to live with a man who is willfully conscious.

216

He who lives in consciousness does not put love first because he knows that this emotion is ephemeral. Women have told me they loved me after two weeks of seeing each other, and then after two months they break it off cataclysmically because they find the idea that I want other women in my life unbearable. So that's why I take my time before considering a woman my partner. I let them get wound up, telling me fifty times a day that they love me, but I won't reciprocate unless I truly feel love for them. People often confuse love and passion. Two years seem to be a reasonable time to allow the blinding dust of passion to fall back to Earth. At this point in my life, I want to invest in relationships of an energetic essence that will pass the test of death. That does not prevent me from remaining open to new women in my life. I trust my system. I don't get carried away and I take the time to become friends with my partners.

217

With me, it's guaranteed emotional schooling. Women who share my love life are constantly confronted by freedom. I bring them back to their feelings and if strong emotions get in the way we observe them together. You can't have a relationship with one who lives in consciousness the same way you would with a person at the first level of thought. With me, there is nothing mechanical; I welcome the unknown without fear, for I see it as an expression of my Being. He who lives in a willfully conscious way is no longer of this world. Those with him must know how to support him when necessary and honor the freedom he represents. When a woman wants to connect with me, I talk to her about freedom. I have her reflect on this subject, implying that if she wants to be my partner, she will have to trust me and let me be free. Love must liberate; it must allow the other to flourish because he feels supported in what he is fundamentally. If a relationship begins thus, in openness, love will grow and resemble compassion more than possession. One cannot aim to be conscious without first realizing that freedom is an integral part of it.

218

To be conscious among an assembly of unconscious minds gives me the impression that I landed in a desert that stretches as far as the eye can see. There is not a soul within a thousand miles. It's perturbing, because at the same time, a dense crowd creates a fuss around me, but it's a crowd of ghosts that do not exist. Fortunately, I have managed to gather around me a solid core of people who live consciously like me or aspire to with all their might. It reassures me to know that this planet is not a lost cause. I wouldn't go so far as to say that there is hope, but maybe miracles do exist. I am generous toward those who seem to deserve my attention. I give them a little of my Being in order to set in motion the self-movement of their own Being. It's a bit like recharging the dead battery of a car whose driver is a friend. It is very satisfying to hear his car start again.

219

With time, I have come to systematically add consciousness to everything I do. It's the magic ingredient I can sprinkle everywhere and that allows me to operate the miraculous. Everything is a pretext to bring me back to my center, like a metaphysical game whose aim is to to keep me open to my eternal essence. Every day I am awed by simple things that enchant me and make my life pleasant, like gliding quietly on a peaceful lake. It is the feeling that stands out from all others at the moment. Everything is going to pot around me; people are incredibly ignorant and constantly get in trouble. And I observe all this impassively; my life is charmed and always has been. I don't understand the extent to which people make their own lives difficult. When I feel an opening I may share some of my Being with these shadows I encounter. I light them from the inside; I give them a chance to feel my Being. Most of the time it leads to nothing; as soon as I leave their sight, they fall back into their mechanical and soulless life. I feel, nonetheless, that I have planted a seed that will grow one day if everything is put in place for them to awaken. It does not require much energy; in truth, I do not try to convince them rationally. I am beyond that. I am content to be a humble example. I offer them a touch of Being without expecting anything in return. What motivates me is the pleasure of seeing their eyes light up as something unknown to them, unintelligible, passes through them. This is the attitude of a man who knows he is rich with the substance of the infinite. He first taught himself to receive. This led him to bloom and now he sows his seeds, one by one, wherever his intuition tells him to do so.

220

I have already mentioned that consciousness is a realm of manifestation. This allows me to affirm that the world is in me. This is how I perceive it when I am the Observer. This state of being the Observer is paradoxical because there is no longer an inside or an outside. The world simply "is"; I am this world and I live in it simultaneously. A great openness is required to understand and integrate this because it defies logic. Consciousness having neither an interior nor an exterior cannot be understood rationally, only intuitively. Intuition is my favorite tool. Thanks to it, I feel the invisible with a clairvoyance that never ceases to amaze me. There are so many perceptions I share in my books that are impossible for me to explain to those around me. I am lucky to have developed the gift of writing in order to affirm outside what I feel inside. I feel conscious precisely because I take into account the visible world and bring it back here and make it concrete. In my life, the interior and the exterior mesh so well that I have difficulty separating them. My art is the bridge that allows me to constantly travel between the absolute and the relative.

221

I am so close to everything, and yet I feel so far away. I sometimes see humans as ants. They work on mechanical tasks that support the anthill. I look at them, a little disillusioned, unable to be like them. It was even more pronounced a few years ago when I didn't have a job. At that time, it was incomprehensible to me. I could not fathom why people gave away the majority of their time for a morsel of bread. I already lived in abundance. I had done the calculations: by not spending money on super-fluous things; by having no desire to travel, amuse myself, have a house or a car, I could live cheaply. I made use of food banks, bought my clothes in thrift shops and found my furniture on the sidewalk. In short, I lived on the abundance of the infinite. I did not call it that at the time but I felt free to finally Be. I had no fixed schedule, no alarm to jolt me awake at seven in the morning. I got used to seeing the world from an elevated point of view that gave me an unusual depth of perception. It is this state of creative idleness that fixed in me the absolute. I was like the Greeks who invented philosophy. You need time to think, and for ten years I gave myself twenty-four hours a day. Not having much money made me pay attention to all the details. I could not afford to lose my apartment or buy useless things. I had to filter all my desires to judge which ones were mine and which ones were those perniciously imposed on me by society.

222

Having all the time in the world for ten years fostered in me a closeness with everything around me. I was part of the world, always attentive to my intuition. On the other hand, those who work like mules live at full speed and spend huge sums on things that make them look good. I have a job now. It is a conscious choice I made a few years ago. But I have kept this feeling of being detached from the world populated by unconscious workers. I work in the world in a willfully conscious way. I do what my Being gives me to do but without identifying myself with it. This inevitably leads me to where I am supposed to be.

223

Being conscious means having to always stay open. It isn't easy, but I make it a practice, and in time the satisfaction it provides justifies continuing this way. Today we are reminded incessantly about the dangers of sexually transmitted diseases. It's enough to make you paranoid. But if I fall into this trap—if I begin to distrust all women who come to me—how can I ask them to be open and confident with me and my ideas? Openness is a fundamental quality of one who lives in consciousness. How could it be otherwise, once the world has become clear and intelligible? Unfortunately, this is not common today. Talk about sex for a minute and you quickly understand that the manipulative plutocratic system has managed to associate the word "sex" with "STD." It is sometimes hard to bear for me, who would rather associate sex with openness and communion. How do you communicate with someone who is afraid of you from the start, someone you protect yourself from when you make love? I believe that the first impression is the right one. So I make it my duty to be open when a new woman wants to be in a relationship with me. I know that if she is infected my Being will warn me subtly.

224

Please, don't to talk to me about consciousness
if you are not able to stay open! I often meet
people who do energy work like reiki or Ayur-
veda, and when I tell them that I make love
without protection, they become tense and parrot the first level man's speech that I may get
STDs. I can understand that ordinary people
may think so—they are ignorant people who
have no discernment—but it seems to me that
someone who dedicates his life to healing others
at the most subtle levels should understand.
And yet, many people will do their yoga, work
with energy, but when it comes time to show
that they are one with the ideas they peddle,
suddenly they become pure materialists again.
I am always surprised when I meet this type
of person; they are dangerous liars. As for me,
I persist in remaining open and trusting my
Being. So the next time you have a discussion with this type of person ask them if they
wear a condom when they make love. If they
answer "yes" ask them to specify if they wear
one because they do not want children or so as
not to catch STDs. Their answer will say a lot
about who they are and how well they integrate
their ideas on the human plane. We do not catch
diseases on the physical level, we give them to
ourselves on the subtle level... every conscious
being knows that.

225

Can you imagine Jesus Christ or Gandhi making
love wearing a condom? It's absurd, isn't it? So,
you who claim to be a sage or a saint, what are

you afraid of? What are you protecting yourself against? The unmistakable quality of one who lives in a willfully conscious way is that he no longer lives in fear. He is not afraid to die or be alone, for he lives in consciousness, which gives him a feeling of permanence. Once I understood this, I stopped protecting myself and surrendered to that part of me that is more myself than my self and that I call Being. You have to know how to trust, that's how you build lasting relationships. I have had brushes with disaster on a few occasions but have always managed to remain one with my ideas. That's what matters most to me. I have the courage to take responsibility for my ideas. I am not a theorist who preaches without applying his principles. Every being divided against himself perishes.

226

In the previous paragraphs I gave you some little tricks to detect the scammers of consciousness. I do not accept the teachings of someone who is not one with his own teachings. He has no credibility in my eyes, and I tell him nicely he can keep his theories to himself. I agree it is not always easy to apply values such as openness, trust and harmony, but what good is it to live in one's head without ever checking in the relative to see if what one believes is true? One must have the courage of one's opinions even if almost no one understands them. I can do without the approbation of others because I have a quiet conscience. I make it my duty to integrate into my daily life the ideas I discuss in my books. He who does not act thus and who prides himself on living in consciousness risks experiencing a very painful moment at the hour of his death, for he will be confronted with the truth of what he is and not of what he repeated like a parrot all his life, without understanding its basis.

227

Discernment is not necessarily acquired with age, but with consciousness. Today, many people are interested in consciousness. They greet you by joining their hands like Hindus and giving you a "Namaste." They make efforts to be fashionable, to speak to you of the East as the Promised Land, but they are so hypnotized by this distant ideal that they forget their own culture. This is a fine example of a lack of judgment. They let themselves be decentered by techniques that have nothing to do with their own essence because, deep down, they know they won't have the desired results. They are restless and don't know what's good for them. They embark on a difficult path that they will abandon after a few years for lack of tangible results, and especially for lack of a context conducive to the development of consciousness. This seems to me the most violent lack of judgment, because it is directed against oneself. I know that I risk offending numerous people who will recognize themselves in this description. Know that I am simply noting a wild certainty: enlightenment passes through the person. If I am a Westerner, the smartest is for me to adopt a practice with a Western flavor. I can spice it with orientalism, as long as it remains an embellishment and a way of enlivening it. But at my core, I remain a Westerner and if I want to remain conscious among the horde of unconscious, I must use what I Am.

228

It is difficult to judge others well when we have heard incessantly since childhood platitudes like "we must not judge others." On the contrary, others must be judged quickly and accurately. It is easier to stop a leech than try to pull it off once it has its fangs firmly planted in our flesh. It is a principle which seems obvious but is rarely put into practice. More than three thousand years of propaganda has gotten the upper hand on intelligence, but an instinctive and innate form remains. Animals do not ask themselves questions of a moral nature. They know instantly whether a person is good or bad. Humans have perfected the art of lying, though, so it is true that it is often difficult to judge them, but this is precisely where consciousness comes into play. We must learn to make use of its transparency to give us access to the invisible. In short, it is not with the mind that we judge, but with intuition. Still, we must have enough confidence to follow our intuition when it tells us the opposite of what our mind tells us. Those who will survive the great changes that will soon strike humanity will be those who will be able to judge quickly and accurately a situation or a new encounter. Escalating events will soon bring change. Those who do not have this ability will inevitably find themselves in the wrong place at the wrong time. Contrary to what the Church has told us, judging, and above all judging well, is a great quality.

229

I live in a willfully conscious way because I feel it is the only worthwhile way to live. I am not ashamed to judge people. I even practice it with a relish that grows every time my initial intuition is confirmed by the facts. I make an effort not to tack my fears on others, though. This isn't always easy because my intellect is rather robust and could easily overwhelm me had I not developed clever tricks to not accept logical reasoning passively. I understand that my thinking shapes the world and people will tend to act like I presume they will. If I'm afraid someone will steal from me, it's very likely that that person will do so... just to confirm what I think. But this often has nothing to do with the first impression, which was quickly forgotten. If you manage to fix this first impression by making it conscious, then you will be guided wisely in your interaction with others. The conscious man knows. He has a first impression and fixes it at the center of his relationship with others. He is not mistaken, because in the invisible all is clear and given to those who are ready to receive.

230

I fix my thoughts' horizon to grasp what I need to know every moment. My intellect is, on the other hand, occupied in performing tasks of the moment and foreseeing those coming. So I cannot trust it to see what is beyond the linear world. On the horizon appear wild certainties that I accept with an ease that sometimes shocks my intellect. But I learned to master the latter so it doesn't harm me. I harnessed my folly so that it serves me instead of slowing me down in useless conjuncture. Wild certainties are beyond proof; they content themselves to be. Since I Am, too, it's easy for me to make myself one with them and let them guide me to the right place at the right time. The universe is finely tuned and a second of hesitation can be fatal. The horizon is the infinite; when I truly contemplate it I become more perceptive because it brings me back by analogy to this fundamental state which is more my self than myself: the absolute.

231

This thought horizon is not a place but rather a state of being. It serves as a reference for me to convert to what I Am. It is a springboard from which I launch my self into myself without constraint. I am a contemplative. It is therefore natural for me to focus on this part of me that is vast and unbound. I find my best ideas there because they are not of this world. I have understood that this thought horizon is the gateway to the world of ideas of which Plato spoke. I feel at home here.

232

There came a point in my life when I began to ask myself serious questions about reality and consciousness. I read compulsively everything

I could get my hands on. I came to understand what others were saying: thinkers, philosophers, sages, saints and so on. But I only really understood when I had my first mystical experience. It was then that I realized that you don't understand consciousness, you experience it. And it was this experience in conjunction with an intellectual understanding of it that allowed me to integrate consciousness into my life. I then found that part of me that is more myself than my self. A series of other experiences followed and lead me to gradually abdicate. All those false ideas that had been imposed upon me since childhood were challenged, and all those with no real foundation were discarded. It is true that, unlike most people, I was willing to do anything to free myself. I wanted to push my luck to its most extreme limit, risk everything and rid myself once and for all of all those programs I had never really believed. If a person is not ready to lose everything to have the pleasure of living in consciousness, he will never succeed. In this realm, it's all or nothing.

233

Consciousness will always remain out of the grasp of those who still cling to their physical envelope and possessions, for as soon as they begin to feel their Being vibrate, they recognize that it is to the detriment of everything that they possess in this world. Being gets us used to living in permanence, and nothing in this world is permanent, except consciousness. This is the ultimate challenge: divesting from the world while remaining in it. It implies appreciating those you love while keeping in mind that they are just passing through your consciousness. It means that even your self is just passing. Living in a willfully conscious way causes you to relax, let yourself be and let others be. It is an attitude that my cats have led me to understand. A cat's life is much shorter than mine, so it's obvious they will die before I do. The coup de grace came a year ago when my year-and-a-half-old kitten was hit by a car in front of my house. This incident re-enforced my awareness that life is ephemeral and that a being that I love may not come back if I set it free. I am not one of those who require a contract to undertake a romantic relationship. I tell myself that if I leave my loved one free to come and go, I have a better chance of knowing her true feelings. So, I trust myself because I have developed in me a boundless source of pleasure, which every day becomes more and more perceptible. I am not afraid of being alone; my thoughts keep me company. And since I am free from this fear of being alone, I appreciate the people close to me more, for I keep the perspective of infinity in the relationships I weave with them. I seek to actuate in them that desire for permanence which alone can lead them to forge a partnership with me based on values that promote awareness. This is how I live in a willfully conscious way, by sharing eternity with friends of my essence.

234

An unbearable metaphysical irritation arose in me two weeks ago. Over the last few months, a tension had accumulated to reach this breaking point, and the only solution I could see was to bring it to consciousness—extirpate it from me to better dissociate myself from it. I wrote pages of the second part of this book every day and I finally found peace. The source of irritation did not disappear, but I changed radically. As a result, friends of my essence were drawn closer to me through an irresistible force. They came to me and recounted the dreams they had of me over the last two weeks. They were strangely consistent with what I experienced since I began writing this book again. Other people were pushed away. They were saddled with problems and situations that had nothing to do with what I Am. Creative violence is like this. It lifts me, loosens my binds and brings me where I am supposed to be. I never resist it because it is my best friend.

235

Consciousness is not acquainted with compromise because it is everything and has nothing to lose. It is therefore normal that he who applies himself to living in a willfully conscious way comes to abide in a serene state devoid of anguish. Continuity is stronger than all fears. And like the waves of the ocean that buffet the shore relentlessly, consciousness can soften even the most brutal of men if they abandon themselves to it. A great anger rises in me sometimes. I look at it attentively because I know it could destroy me or ruin my life. I witness it and let my quality of artist help it pass and fix itself in the relative to become tangible enough that I can transcend it. I know too well that my thoughts shape the world around me and that if I allow the most violent of them to simply pass, they will soften and I will be able to use them as fertilizer to create beauty. Thanks to art, I sublimate those forces of nature which have overwhelmed so many. It is because I live in consciousness that I can harness my folly and use it for the good of my community.

236

I feel a mighty power unfolding in me. It intimidates me sometimes because I fear destroying things without intending to. I feel like an elephant in a china shop. Each of my movements might upend something or someone too fragile. There are so many victims in our society! It is a real epidemic. This constant lamenting exhausts me. I am naturally sweet and good but at times it is very difficult not to explode. I have this recurring dream of a domesticated lion that follows me everywhere, as my cats do. Except that in this case, a wild beast could injury me with an offhand swipe of a paw. I know this lion represents my feeling of being too strong for the majority. I am very dominant and the power that unfolds in me could turn against me if I am not completely attentive. I sometimes scratch people I come in contact with but I can't say I ever attacked anyone gratuitously. My strength is contained, domesticated, so to speak, but it retains its destructive potential that can't be ignored. Luckily, I live in a willfully conscious manner. In this way, I can witness myself and keep a tight rein on this power potential. It is also fortunate that I am a writer and artist, which allows me to make all of these unfounded fears conscious. I am more serene at last, but when I started writing the second part of this book two weeks ago, I was at the breaking point. The anger that rose in me could have floored me or made me sick. I spoke recently to friends who experienced something similar. They dreamt of me, but did not have the intelligence or the ability to handle the anger and got sick. As for me, I released the tension by examining it through writing and here I am again in peace. There will certainly be other sources of irritation—we're not short of them down here— but I know I will have the wisdom not to react, to sit in a corner and to write down my feelings as clearly as possible to make them conscious.

237

What characterizes conscious life is a clear sense of freedom. I feel free on all levels and this is reflected in my everyday life. I am free because I am complete. I am not dependent on anything because my center of balance is in me. I do not depend on anyone, as much in my work as in love and friendship. If I lose a client, two more usually come knocking the same week. I constantly use my intelligence to diversify myself, so as not to be obliged to do something I don't want to. This feeling of freedom began in my earliest childhood. I still hear my father say that he let us be free. I agree with him on this point; he managed to make freedom a habit in my life. He who lives in a willfully conscious way is free because he understands that everything in this world is ephemeral and that he must love without holding anybody back or making them a prisoner. Underlying all my actions is the desire to teach others to be free. I prefer my companions to feel free so that if they want to share my life, they do so of their own accord and not because we have signed a contract. I can do that because I feel bountiful and limitless. I do not need anyone to be happy, but I appreciate the presence of those I love, while keeping in mind that they are only just passing before my consciousness, which is immutable.

238

How can I not feel free when I recognize the absolute in everything? I am joyful and what predominates in my life is a feeling of profound freedom. It comes through in my work. I have always given myself great creative freedom. The current society may be stifling and narrow, but I have always had the gift to sneak through the cracks in the system. I have used it to amuse myself and work as little as possible. Those who are imprisoned in complicated situations are not intelligent. I go through life consciously, and with every step I take I make sure not to fall into a trap that would impose unwanted responsibilities on me. I teach my clients to be self-sufficient so that they call on me only when necessary. I do not want to hold them hostage. Many web designers also offer site hosting and assume responsibility if there is a problem. I offered this service to a few customers but I quickly realized that it was too much responsibility. I never lose sight of the fact that my ultimate goal is to live by my art and not to serve others; I want to be useless. If, however, I can help others because I have such and such a skill, I am happy to do so if I feel inspired. I understand that all this is only a pretext to enter into relation with others. I find the absolute in my work as a graphic designer. At times, I experience an orgasmic pleasure in pushing my limits to please my clients, knowing well that my work is so close to my nature as an artist that I can always use the knowledge thus acquired in my art. I am so in harmony with what I have set out to be that I freely commit myself to each project offered to me.

239

Joy-energy-freedom-consciousness: it is in this quaternity that I can live in a willfully conscious way. I endeavor to feel these four aspects of my Being in everything. These four words are less loaded with enmity than the word "God," so often I prefer to use them to describe the state in which I Am.

240

I am blessed. I am conscious of living in a state that is unintelligible to most. How I understand Christ and the Buddha! They are friends of my essence... they and all those who have created a permanent center of gravity and crossed over to infinity with their eyes open. My state is similar to these men who have rebalanced the energy here below. "What pretension!" will bellow the least imaginative. It should not be forgotten that over time myth distances itself more and more from its source. Thus, in two thousand years, I will be seen very differently than today. My defects will be forgotten, as will the fact that I sometimes spent more time thinking than Being. As for me, I am already conscious of what I Am. What differentiates me from others is so subtle that it is perceptible to almost no one. But those who are close to me understand better what I express. The mediums, the sages and the saints converge towards me because they feel an affinity. In my presence, they feel understood and appreciated. I am humble despite everything. I do not need others to confirm that I Am. All the signs confirm this. All I do is imbibed with consciousness. I apply myself to being good at all times because I know that what a man is speaks louder than what he says.

241

What does the word family mean for the one who lives in consciousness? There is certainly a familiarity in those we call our family, but on Earth this word seems somewhat absurd. That's why I came to differentiate between the elected family and the biological family. Here below, the biological family is rarely also the elected family. We enter the world in an ephemeral family with whom we share almost nothing except blood and physical traits. Living in the permanence of energy, I find it hard to consider those with whom I grew up part of my elected family because they live only in the emotional. I love them with all my heart, don't get me wrong, but I know that they are only passing through. On the other hand, those in whom I see consciousness manifest seem to me really familiar; we can share eternity together. It is rare that I have this feeling; those who live consciously are very few in number. When I meet this kind of enlightened being, I know that nothing else matters except to be attentive to them. If I look behind me, I see the people who were important in my life and they seem so far away now. They resemble cartoon characters. I see no desire on their part to fix the absolute in themselves or break the infernal cycle of reincarnation. Personally, I am not resigned to dying just because everybody else is.

242

I am getting comfortable loving without holding the other back. I like to teach others to be free so that once released, they can consciously decide to stay in my life. Let no one speak to me of those jealous husbands who imprison their wives so as not to lose them. For me, that's just the beginning of the end. I don't want to lie to myself. I don't want false relationships. Nothing resists consciousness; those who want to be with me are forced to live consciously, too... I don't leave them the choice. When a woman remains in my life despite the truth that I willfully provoke in her, I know then that our relationship is not just emotional, but energetic. Those who think only of establishing themselves forever in their center will find in me a faithful friend. It is so rare to meet mature beings sensitive enough to appreciate what I Am. That is why I cling with all my strength to my permanent center of gravity. I do not want to let myself be decentered by all these love beggars. I am well aware they are just passing because what I have to offer is very different. My gift to those I love is to teach them to do without me, for it is only at this point that an authentic relationship of an energetic essence begins: on the threshold of freedom. I teach, in fact, to live in a willfully conscious way.

THE END